TWAYNE'S WORLD AUTHORS SERIES

A Survey of the World's Literature

Sylvia E. Bowman, Indiana University
GENERAL EDITOR

SPAIN

Gerald Wade, Vanderbilt University
EDITOR

José María Gironella

(TWAS 164)

TWAYNE'S WORLD AUTHORS SERIES (TWAS)

The purpose of TWAS is to survey the major writers —novelists, dramatists, historians, poets, philosophers, and critics—of the nations of the world. Among the national literatures covered are those of Australia, Canada, China, Eastern Europe, France, Germany, Greece, India, Italy, Japan, Latin America, the Netherlands, New Zealand, Poland, Russia, Scandinavia, Spain, and the African nations, as well as Hebrew, Yiddish, and Latin Classical literatures. This survey is complemented by Twayne's United States Authors Series and English Authors Series.

The intent of each volume in these series is to present a critical-analytical study of the works of the writer; to include biographical and historical material that may be necessary for understanding, appreciation, and critical appraisal of the writer; and to present all material in clear, concise English—but not to vitiate the scholarly content of the work by doing so.

José María Gironella

By RONALD SCHWARTZ

City University of New York

Twayne Publishers, Inc.   ::   New York

For my lovely wife Amelia
and our beautiful son Jonathan Fletcher

Preface

José María Gironella is a successful novelist currently living in Spain. He achieved a reputation as a popular novelist there and abroad chiefly because of his novels that treat of the Spanish Civil War. These are the well-known trilogy—*The Cypresses Believe in God*, *One Million Dead* and *The Peace Has Broken Out* (this last volume soon to be translated into English). It is both difficult and rewarding to assess the life and works of a living writer whose career is in constant evolution. This book is meant as an analysis of Gironella's entire literary production to date. Its aim is to show how the writer has progressed from amateur to experienced artist; there is sought the explication of the spiritual correlation between the man and his literary creations, his ideas on art, religion, his country, himself, and the world at large. It is convenient, therefore, to consider his publications in the chronological order of their composition.

It is difficult to place a popular writer such as Gironella in a literary category which both indicates the influences that have shaped his work and reflects his development as a novelist. Therefore, one must judge of his literary output by an examination of his style, his particular mode of perception, and the importance of the literary themes he chooses. It is the ultimate aim of this book to encourage the reader to take up the multi-faceted works of Gironella in order to reach a full understanding of his talents, the man, and his view of contemporary Spain.

Gironella is placed as a transitional figure of the "Generation of 1939" post-Civil War writers with tendencies of the "Generation of 1950." For the material of his novels he relies heavily on his personal experiences: his fiction thus becomes in part an expression of his own personality. His critical spirit and liberal attitude exert a strong influence on contemporary Spain. This attitude is one of the major traits of his personality that give dimension and breadth to Gironella's career as novelist, social critic, political theorist, and historian. I propose to study Gironella in these contexts. Although I acknowledge my indebtedness to critical and biographical materials which have appeared over the years since the beginning of his career, my main source of gratitude is to the author himself. During the long interview he permitted me at his summer home in Arenys de Mar (Barcelona) on August 3, 1965, Gironella revealed himself, correcting, corroborating, criticizing, questioning, challenging, and sometimes changing my points of view about his life and work. I have utilized my notes from this interview to provide information where little or none existed before about the author's life and work.

The reader who takes up this book will also realize that special attention is paid to the Civil War trilogy since the war itself is the crucial experience of Gironella's life. These novels reveal Gironella's use of realism to explicate in graphic terms the panorama and problems of the Spanish Civil War. I have quoted extensively from these novels, translating my selections into English from these works as well as all others treated in this study. I have offered plot outlines in minimal form, preferring instead to develop Gironella's understanding of himself and of the world culture of which he is an important part. Like all master storytellers, Gironella is unique in many ways. Although not all of his works have been received by critics and readers with equal appreciation, they are without exception fascinating explorations of the contemporary Spanish scene by a writer endowed with unusual and rewarding perspectives.

RONALD SCHWARTZ

City University of New York

Acknowledgments

I would like to express my deepest appreciation to Professors Robert E. Osborne and Carlos A. Pérez of the University of Connecticut and Dr. John O. H. Stigall of the City University of New York for their advice and encouragement during the preparation of this book.

I am indebted to José María Gironella for granting me an interview and opening his life and library to me.

I am grateful for the assistance of Mrs. Diana Blaikie without whose help this manuscript would not have been completed so quickly.

I am thankful to my parents, my brother, and my wife for their comfort and patience during the composition of this book.

Contents

Chronology

1917   December 31: José María Gironella born in Darnius (Gerona).

1917–   Years of childhood and adolescence in Darnius. Ambitions
1936   to be a priest. Works as day laborer, factory apprentice.

1935–   Works as bank clerk at Arús Bank in Gerona on eve of
1936   Civil War.

1936–   Begins to write love poetry. Joins Nationalist Army and
1939   serves with ski patrol at Huesca.

1940   Returns to Gerona and becomes newspaper reporter, editor.

1942   Works as correspondent for Italian newspaper *Informazione* in Rome.

1945   Publishes his first love poem "Ha llegado el invierno y tú
        no estás aquí" ("Winter Has Come and You Are Not
        Here").

1946   Wins Nadal Prize for his first novel, *Un hombre*, translated as *Where the Soil Was Shallow*, and marries his
        childhood sweetheart Magda.

1947–   Gironella and wife leave Spain illegally and travel in
1952   France, Italy, Austria, and Sweden.

1949   Publishes his second novel *La marea* (*The Tide*).

1951–   Suffers nervous breakdown in Paris and seeks cures at
1953   various clinics in Vienna and Helsinki while completing
        his first novel of the Spanish Civil War trilogy.

1953   *Los cipreses creen en Dios* (*The Cypresses Believe in
        God*) is published and becomes an instantaneous international best seller.

1954   Gironella publishes a short treatise on the art of writing
        novels entitled *El novelista ante el mundo* (*The Novelist
        Before the World*), written in response to the success of
        The Cypresses.

1958   *Los fantasmas de mi cerebro* (*Phantoms of My Brain*) documents the symptoms of Gironella's nervous breakdown.

1959– Gironella makes his first trip to New York, Cuba (during
1960   the Castro Revolution), and Mexico.

1961   Writes *Todos somos fugitivos* (*We Are All Fugitives*), his first attempt at the short story, completes the second volume of the Spanish Civil War trilogy (*Un millón de muertos* (*One Million Dead*), and works on a short novel.

1962   Publishes *Mujer, levántate y anda* (*Woman, Arise and Walk*).

1962– Gironella and his wife make two trips to the Orient.
1964

1964   *Personas, ideas y mares* (*Persons, Ideas and Seas*) is a book of miscellaneous essays published as a result of Gironella's trip to India, Ceylon, and Egypt. *El Japón y su duende* (*Japan and Her Ghosts*) is an account of his trip there with friend Narciso Yepes, famous Catalan guitarist.

1965   August 3: Gironella is interviewed by Ronald Schwartz at his summer home in Arenys de Mar (Barcelona). Later that year, his book *China, lágrima innumerable* (*China, Countless Tears*) is published.

1965– Gironella works on last volume of Spanish Civil War tril-
1966   ogy *Ha estallado la paz* (*The Peace Has Broken Out*), published late in 1966.

1967   Gironella writes another collection of essays *Gritos del Mar* (*Shouts from the Sea*), a successor to *Persons, Ideas and Seas*.

1968   Gironella vacations at Benidorm in summer and is hard at work on new novel tentatively entitled *Los hombres lloran solos* (*Men Cry Alone*), a sequel to the Civil War trilogy which he hopes to expand. *En Asia se muere bajo las estrellas* (*In Asia You Die Under the Stars*) appears early in this year, a successor to his last travel book *Japan and Her Ghosts*.

CHAPTER 1

Gironella's Life, Times and Literary Creed

I *The Historical and Cultural Background*

JUSTIFIABLY, Gironella has been called a post-Civil War writer belonging to what has been labeled the Generation of 1939. He began to write steadily after the Spanish Civil War and published his first novel, *Un hombre* (*Where the Soil Was Shallow*), in 1946, winning the Nadal Prize. A brief review of literary developments in Spain since 1900 is necessary to appreciate its importance.

A. *The Spanish Novel Before Gironella*

Although the nineteenth century had been a politically and economically chaotic one for Spain, literature had flourished with the successive developments of Romanticism, Costumbrism, and the Regional, the Realist, and Naturalist novels. After rebelling against the formalism of the eighteenth century, the Romantic writers of the early 1800's utilized their newly won individual freedoms to express their emotional natures, their deepest personal feelings, their "unhibited" egos all in keeping with the romantic ideals of life and love. *Costumbrista* authors, reacting to the extremes of Romanticism, captured the folkloric attitudes of Spaniards and with charm and wit often satirized traditions of the provinces. However, it was not until Fernán Caballero wrote in mid-century the first "sociological" novel, with its descriptions of typical towns and villages that the Regional novel was established in Spain and paved the way for the later Realist writers, who described with vivid accuracy both the beauty and the ugliness of rural and city life. Realist novelists such as Juan Valera and Pérez Galdós re-created in detail the urban milieus of nineteenth-century Spanish society, their social turmoil and many problems. Naturalist writers such as Clarín and Pardo Bazán built upon the success of the Realist authors, showing the

15

sordid aspects of Spanish life in minute detail, and, at times, sought reforms of social institutions.

A short but brilliant period followed in which a new group of writers, such as Ganivet, Unamuno and Azorín, known as the Generation of 1898, sought to give new directions to Spanish literature. They broke with the past, offered a diagnosis of what they saw as Spain's cultural and moral decay. However, it was the Modernist doctrine of Rubén Darío that most influenced the young writers of the early 1900's.

At the turn of the century, the Spanish novel was preoccupied with the Modernist ideals: a sensitivity to art and beauty, Romantic individualism, a fascination for the strangely beautiful or exotic and an international audience. Modernism was primarily a literary movement affecting many of Europe's leading writers. It evolved between 1916 and 1924 and has been one of the most influential literary movements of the Generation of 1939.

World War I upset Spain's spiritual, moral and aesthetic orientation. With the collapse of bourgeois social institutions, many European authors gave free rein to their creative abilities, subscribing to a series of new European literary formulas which were properly known as the "isms"—Creationism, Dadaism, Ultraism, Surrealism, etc. Some Spanish writers embraced Vicente Huidobro's Creationist doctrine which stressed unlimited freedom for the creative poet. For Huidobro, the poet was a God who had the power to create an entire world. Others favored Ultraism, an artistic movement whose members sought to sever all ties with their tradition, concentrating on contemporary themes for the content of their works. They created "pure works" of fiction or poetry which attempted to express the inexpressible. Ramón Gómez de la Serna intensified the aims of the Ultraists' quest for "pure art" when he became leader of the Surrealist trend in Spain. The Surrealists tried to uncover hidden truths of thought through an exploration of man's imagination and psyche by combining the nihilistic and infantile spirit of Tristán Tzara's Dadaist movement with psychoanalysis.

Many Spanish novelists of this era rejected the tradition of the nineteenth-century Realist novels of Clarín and Galdós in favor of analyses of their own sensations, emotions, and ideas in response to these fashionable literary styles, the vogue of Paris and Madrid between 1919 and 1928.[1] The great literary critic

Ortega y Gasset recognized that the European novel of the 1920's suffered an excess of intellectualism, seriously debilitating the imaginative powers of the novelist and paralyzing the genre.[2] Consequently, he held that the novelists of the 1920's wrote few fictional works of lasting quality because they subordinated the realities of the exterior world to personal fantasy and thematic content based largely on what he saw as trivia. Therefore, such stylistic "exercises" made little contribution toward advancing the genre.

Despite the appeal and excesses of these writers, several novelists continued to write in the Spanish tradition of nineteenth-century Realism. Although thematic content varied in their individual works, they emphasized certain nationalistic values rather than the new cosmopolitanism. These conservative authors became known as the "Generation of 1923" and were disciples of Galdosian Realism. Their novels dealt with the psychological aspects of man's nature. The early works of Ramón Sender are exemplary of a return to writing novels in the tradition of nineteenth-century Realism.

With the outbreak of civil war in 1936, the majority of Spanish novelists abandoned their dedication to "pure art" which had vitiated an approach to the social and historic realities of the late 1920's and early 1930's. Politically active, they embraced Communism, Fascism, or some other current political ideology. Thus the Civil War not only interrupted the normal development of the Realist writers but placed them in opposing political camps. Some lived harmoniously under the Nationalist policies of Franco. Others who defended Republican Spain were forced into exile after the war.

All Spanish literature, irrespective of genre, suffered a division of creative effort as a consequence of the war. The emigrants, who resided chiefly in Latin America, tried to reestablish their literary reputations. Through the bitterness of their defeat and in exile, they attempted to elucidate the reasons for the war. The novels of Ramón Sender, Arturo Barea, and Francisco Ayala exemplify this particular current. However, in Spain itself, a new generation of young writers concerned with the traumatic effects of the war, and living under Franco's Nationalist regime, engendered the true resurgence of the Spanish novel. Many of these younger writers remember the war and some participated

in it. Reviving the Realist tradition of nineteenth-century novelists, their novels dealt with social themes of contemporary Spanish society and the Civil War. They utilized documentary and
photographic evidence and some cultivated new forms of the
novel as a stylistic outgrowth of the mechanical and dehuman-
ized techniques of the writers of the 1920's. The *novela-reportaje*
or essayistic novel is an example of such a new novel. Other writers proved their manifold skills by writing sociological treatises,
literary criticism or highly stylized works in which they
created an entirely new aesthetic. Camilo José Cela's *tremendismo* is an example of a new aesthetic evolved as the result of
an attempt to reproduce contemporary reality from a personal,
profound, graphic, and highly stylized basis. Some novelists
combined fantastic motifs with reality, exoticism with mundane
themes. Others seriously portrayed their war experiences autobiographically or semiautobiographically. Still others attempted
to reproduce reality photographically, describing their experiences in the new realm of realistic perception tempered by the
Surrealist's sensibility. Some of their qualities are found among
the new "Generation of 1939" writers, of whom José María
Gironella is most assuredly a member.

B. *Gironella and the Developing Spanish Novel*

Gironella revived the Spanish tradition of nineteenth-century
Realism. His novels represent a break from the introspective,
aesthetic and intellectualized pre-Civil War novel. The trauma
of his Civil War experiences caused his return to Realism and to
the exterior world with its imperative political and social problems. Gironella is a serious writer, living in Spain, who reflects
both his personal traumatic experiences of the war and the realities of postwar Spain in his work.

Since Gironella began publishing in 1945, a new generation
of writers has arisen—the "Generation of 1950." Never having
known the fears or dangers of the Civil War, they continue the
realist trend in fiction in social novels. Whereas the 1939 generation of novelists described the social significance of their era, the
"Generation of 1950" writers preferred to act as critics, denounc-
ing the effects of the present regime. Carmen Laforet, Camilo
José Cela, Juan Goytisolo, among others, utilizing the contributions of the "Generation of 1939" writers, have reduced the de-

scriptive element in their works. Their creations are sober, direct works which, deceptive in their simplicity, suggest a number of undeveloped themes. While Gironella may exhibit those characteristics that probably categorize him as a "Generation of 1939" novelist, his subsequent literary efforts have been equally formative and susceptible to these newer intellectual currents. Consequently, his consistent flexibility demonstrates the author's formation and assimilation of the new watchwords of the "Generation of 1950" novelists. He may also be considered a member of this group. Saínz de Robles sums up succinctly some of the new characteristics of the 1950 writers:

. . . realism, objectivity, description, a documentary style in their colloquial and exacting use of language. They share an abhorrence of metaphor, of paradox, of the subtle poetic image and of feelings of eroticism without their complexities or delights. In portraying these qualities, the writers of the 1950's use a coldly written style, almost scientific. Their comprehension of beings and of things depend only upon their attraction to a particular temperament, on their laborious studies of submissive or inverted mentalities and on their pretensions to portray excited psychological states in sensitive, exasperated personalities.[3]

At first glance of the author's career, Gironella's virtuosity in a multiplicity of genres is indicative of his refusal to submit to Spain's literary paralysis. In fact, the brilliance of Gironella's literary career which already spans two "literary" generations and may possibly help to engender a third, may be revealed either as a commentary upon modern man or upon Gironella, the writer constantly in search of himself.

II *Gironella's Life*

José María Gironella was born in Darnius, a small fishing village near Gerona on December 31, 1917, and is proud of his Catalan heritage. He wanted to be a priest but abandoned this chiefly because of his self-doubt. He worked at a series of odd jobs, such as a ragman, factory apprentice, bank clerk, store proprietor, book salesman, newspaper reporter and editor. Like his hero Ignacio Alvear in *Los cipreses creen en Dios* (*The Cypresses Believe in God*), the author found himself caught in Gerona working in the Arús Bank just at the outbreak of civil war. During the years 1936-39, he fought with the Nationalists and served

at Huesca with a battalion of ski soldiers on the peaks of the
Pyrenees. When the war ended, Gironella returned to Gerona in
1940. No longer content with his position at the bank, and with
an irresistible urge to write, he became a newspaper reporter
and contributed a variety of articles to many journals and magazines. He also worked as a correspondent for the newspaper
Informazione in Rome. Shortly thereafter, he married his long-
time sweetheart Magda whom he had met at a dance in Gerona.
Gironella soon found that the restrictive narrowness of Spanish
provincial life was difficult for the development of his productive
powers and left Spain for a wider sphere of experience. Magda
Gironella indicates the provincialism of their Catalonian life:
"I couldn't possibly have lived in Gerona after my marriage. It
would have stifled me."[4]

Gironella's publication of his own works began with the appearance of a love poem in 1945. Antonio de Hoyos saw the
beginning of Gironella's literary inspiration thus: "During the
war, he corresponded with thirty-two godmothers, and according
to the novelist's declaration, that was the foundation of his writing career."[5]

Gironella was not to succeed as a poet, but his first novel, *Un
hombre* (*Where the Soil Was Shallow*) won the coveted Nadal
Prize in 1946. Between 1947 and 1952, Gironella and his wife
left Spain illegally and travelled extensively through Europe. He
offered the following explanation of his journey:

A moment comes when one grows tired of seeing the same photographs in the local newspapers and when one determines on a change
of air. I remained abroad until 1952. In the space of these four years
across the highways of Europe, I opened the eyes of my spirit to
learn what I could learn. And in all truth, the gains were, I believe,
considerable. I learned things of capital interest, at least for me. For
instance, I met peopde who talked in a low tone of voice, who pursued truth by means of dialogue, who avoided extreme affirmations.[6]

During this travel period, he wrote in 1949 his second novel,
La marea (*The Tide*). It sold fairly well but was not the artistic
success for which he had hoped. After a nervous breakdown in
1951, while in Paris with his wife, Gironella travelled from clinic
to clinic between Helsinki and Vienna, seeking relief and working as he was able on his next novel. *The Cypresses Believe in*

God, published in 1953, became at once an international best seller. Invited by a group of Finnish publishers to consult upon the translation of this novel, Gironella commented on his decision to leave Spain once again, and now at the peak of his popularity:

Yes, of course I find it difficult to make this decision. But as a writer I feel that I must go. You see, since my illness I have become more restless, more eager to search for new truths, to explore new horizons, to try to understand the ideals, the philosophy, the morality of the world that lies outside the boundaries of my country. For I cannot hope to be objective and unbiased in my writings unless I gain the perspective of distance.[7]

The sequel to *The Cypresses, Un millón de muertos* (*One Million Dead*) which appeared in 1961, was equally successful and reinforced the author's popularity. Between 1953 and 1961 Gironella documented the symptoms of his nervous breakdown, worked toward his mastery of the short story and wrote several serious essays. *Los fantasmas de mi cerebro* (*Phantoms of My Brain*), 1958, and *Todos somos fugitivos* (*We Are All Fugitives*), 1961, are the fruit of these labors. Between 1962 and 1964 the author took his first two trips to the Orient. During these years Editorial Planeta published one novel, *Mujer, levántate y anda* (*Woman, Arise and Walk*), 1962, and two subsequent works documenting his eastern journeys: *Personas, ideas y mares* (*Persons, Ideas and Seas*), 1964, and *El Japón y su duende* (*Japan and Her Ghosts*), 1964. His latest travel book, *China, lágrima innumerable* (*China, Countless Tears*), 1965, is based upon an earlier magazine article. It has been updated and republished because of its particular relevance to Communist China's currently dominant role in East Asia. During the summer of 1965, when I interviewed him at his home in Arenys de Mar, Gironella was hard at work on the third volume of his Civil War trilogy, *Ha estallado la paz* (*The Peace Has Broken Out*), published in Barcelona by Editorial Planeta in 1966, as well as a book of miscellaneous essays.

III   *Gironella's Literary Creed*

Like many young writers, Gironella gave thought to and proposed his own aesthetic; we admire his somewhat amateurish idealism. Although his treatise on the subject is generally unsuccessful because of many generalizations not yet thought through sufficiently, it shows the author's attempt to define his own role as a writer and also serves as an index to the principles of his early novels. An analysis may help us to evaluate Gironella's early works.

It was when Gironella's popularity soared after publication of *The Cypresses Believe in God* that many literary clubs sought him out to lecture about himself and his work. The six chapters of *El novelista ante el mundo* (*Novelist Before the World*) represent a compendium of his ideas adapted from this lecture series. The author has told me, however, that *Novelist* derives mostly from one lecture, delivered on April 11, 1953, at the Ateneo in Madrid.

Gironella opens Chapter One by stating what he considers to be the five cardinal principles indispensable to a novelist: (1) he must be a spiritually solid man and capable as a writer; (2) he must have a strong calling for his profession, be gifted as a writer, and willing to express himself only when he has something important to say; (3) he should belong to a particular geographical area, rooted there intellectually, and delighting in his participation with his clan and its traditions; (4) he must either have analyzed and resolved his personal problems or, if he still is uncertain, he must express his self-doubt and confusion in his writing; and, finally, (5) he must be tenacious, willing to correct and edit, to think of, and live only for, his work. Having understood and accepted these principles, the novelist may now compose a novel. Gironella also defines his idea of what constitutes a novel: ". . . a prolonged, sustained work, one which may constitute for the future a kind of inventory of human feelings."[8]

Chapter Two refines the author's definition of the novelist, reaffirming that he exists within his own world, either nourished or submerged by it. Since daily living impinges dynamically upon the writer, he constantly seeks to understand by means of his curiosity his astonishment, his fear. "The novelist's curiosity is infinite. . . . He is not the man that knows everything, but the man who knows nothing . . ."[9] and attempts to discover meaning in the universe. Astonishment is always present in the novelist's world. "The simplest human actions seem like a mystery to him."[10] Fear causes the novelist continual panic. "He will never be able to understand this fabulous world with only the help of

a pen and an inkstand."[11] Gironella fears that the novelist will be
unable to explain his constant preoccupation with the ephemeral.

Chapter Three considers the roles of hate and love, finding that
both are rooted in fear. Hate and love are the polarities and
initial stimuli that enable the novelist to begin to write. However,
novels conceived in hate are not enduring while those inspired
and nurtured by love are usually superior as artistic creations.
These novels elevate their readers intellectually as they enhance
their sense of beauty and heighten their sensibilities through
perfection of form. Through his novels, transcendental values are
born and sheer pleasure results.

Chapter Four holds that the author's life experiences provide
the material for the novel and that society is a catalyst which
activates the author's five cardinal principles. As society sharpens
the novelist's curiosity and intensifies his astonishment, it increases the novelist's fears. Modern man is increasingly threatened by death as society is now constituted. Consequently, the
novelist writes because of fear tempered by either hate or love
and which he directs at society. The writer who conceives his
work in hate is a novelist of negation. "There are people whose
eyes sparkle when describing pus and those for whom the foetus
is already a corpse..."[12] On the other hand, the novelist who
both hates and loves is the writer who retains some faith in mankind. It is he who is sensitive and talented—in short, the artist.
Gironella defines the artist's outlook in this manner:

[The artist is]... an uninhibited personality for whom walking is, in
a certain sense, dancing, and for whom the attitude of repose is pure
sculpture. The true novelist retains his faith in mankind, in the beauty
of time passing, in solitude or in God. He is the writer who opens
the window and murmurs: "The highest degree of life touches me."[13]

In Chapter Five, Gironella describes the status of Spain's post-
Civil War novelists. Spain has endowed them with ineradicable
motives of curiosity, astonishment, and fear as a consequence of
the nation's complex history. Therefore, Gironella feels the time
is right for the appearance of new men, since the reigning novelists of the Civil War period were reactionary, preferring to
ground themselves in nineteenth-century concepts rather than to
resolve existing problems. The chief literary impetus of the post-
Civil War writers resulted from their astonishment at the erup-

tion of civil war. Curiosity, however, became a perceptible
quality in the novelist's art shortly after 1939. After the Civil
War, Spain's political neutrality was threatened by Communism
on the Left and Western European democracy on the Right.
Gironella believes that the combined forces of political boycott,
drought, and hunger of the pre-World War II period accentuated
the pressures on the Spanish novelist. He doubts the Spaniard
will direct his energies towards work and artistic pursuits intended to nurture the spirit. The very context of Spanish society
has created tremendous fear in the life of the novelists and this
fear is a necessary drive if the Spanish novelist is to create.
Gironella shares this fear with the members of his generation
and it is this fear which prompted him to write.

With the progressive clarification of the Civil War years
through numerous and widely published literary, historical works
and release of film records, Gironella still asserts the serious lack
of creativity in these genres on the part of his contemporaries.
Authors may insist upon clarification of Spain's political tangle
in their novels, but their works do not emphasize their essentially
Spanish nature. If Spanish novelists have failed in their profession, it is because they practice autarchy.

Whatever their shortcomings, Gironella believes that most
Spanish writers cannot be denied talent or patriotism. Wherever
they may travel, they never cut the umbilical cord and Spain is
for them a complete world. Consequently, her novelists never
wander too far from her frontiers. Athough Spanish novelists are
fecund and skilled investigators, they must learn first to conclude
and resolve their personal problems, then the nation's. Nevertheless, parenthetically, Gironella proposes the creation and development of an international ideological exchange in which the
Spaniard can participate in order to help himself and his nation.
However he gives no practical details of how this plan would
work.

Chapter Six prophesies the future for Spain's novelists; Gironella concludes that Spanish writers have acquired, or can acquire
all the qualites needed for success, including narrative talent.
Unfortunately, Gironella believes Spain never developed a large
group of writers who engendered a valuable international inter-
play of ideas. As to government censorship, the author has little
to say because, unlike other Spanish writers, he feels himself

divorced from politics. However, he does believe that the political situation influences the writer's choice of theme and his execution and development of it. In Spain, "to my understanding, this type of censorship alone is decisive and capable enough to frustrate the literary works of my generation."[14] These statements are cautious because of the strict censorship policies of the Spanish government. Because only fourteen years had passed since the Civil War when the author wrote this lecture, he assumed that these policies of General Franco's regime would undergo future revision. Except for censorship of pornographic works, Gironella believed that in the future the Spanish novelist would be virtually free thematically and could legitimately clarify the political tangle of the Civil War years, one of the aims of his generation of writers. Gironella has chosen his words very carefully here, trying not to offend the regime that had let his Civil War novel, *The Cypresses Believe in God*, pass through the rigorous government censorship virtually untouched.

In a final note, he asks his public to humor him because of the highly subjective nature of this literary creed. He has preferred not to develop a series of logical literary principles although *Novelist* may give that distinct impression on occasion. His aim has been to enlighten his public as to the meaning of his own role as a novelist. He does not care to extend the principles contained in this lecture to a full-length critical analysis of Spain's contemporary novelists or novels. *Novelist* is his formulation of a personal code, a working aesthetic in which he says he applies it only to himself. *Novelist*, then, reflects the integrity of a young writer attempting to define his own professional position. The treatise does indeed lack the perception of a mature literary critic. Although Gironella has discovered relatively little that is new about the art of composing a novel or the role of the Spanish novelist in contemporary society, he has determined his own areas of greatest professional competence as demonstrated in his early works.

IV *Principles of* Novelist *as Used in Early Works*

It is apparent that *Novelist Before the World* was written as a direct result of the relative success of his first two novels. The protagonists of *Where the Soil Was Shallow* and *The Tide* in-

carnate many of the principles contained in Gironella's literary
credo. In fact, if we compare the author's commentaries on
Spanish novelists with the characterizations of these protagonists,
we may conclude that these personages embody many of the
principles contained in *Novelist*.

Both male protagonists of *Where the Soil Was Shallow* and
The Tide are intellectually gifted young men, artistically oriented, and living on the periphery of their respective societies.
While Miguel Serra constantly searches for meaning in his life
and a future career throughout Europe in *Where the Soil Was
Shallow*, Adolfo Stolberg of *The Tide* is already an established
architect in Germany. Both suffer spiritual inadequacies, too
much preoccupied with themselves and their own image and,
consequently, frustrate their ambitions for successful careers.
Each has a specific tradition and geographical area. Miguel has
been uprooted from Darnius but tries to justify his European
journeys and eventual return to Spain intellectually as part of a
spiritual regeneration. Adolfo has never left Germany and is a
virtual prisoner there because of his usefulness to the Third Reich
during World War II.

Both men suffer ideological and philosophical confusions. The
chaos and turmoil of their lives provide the action in each novel.
The novels themselves are full of action; they are short but not
very sustained works. Each novel presents an inventory of the
protagonist's feelings *as far as we can know them*. Their characterizations perfectly parallel Gironella's conception of the qualities of the novelist and his definition of the novel as these were
explained on our page 22.

Further, both personages project a spirit of innocence or
naïveté like that which the author professes for himself. Each
operates according to irrepressible curiosities. Both are aston-
ished because of their innocence and suffer great fears leading
them to react in totally different but original ways. Miguel becomes a circus impresario, losing and finding love, the essential
element in his life. Adolfo believes death is the only solution for
the frustration of an uncreative military-oriented architectural
career and a marriage failing because of his wife's infidelity.
Both Miguel and Adolfo seek solutions for their problems as
members of society and both are susceptible to any ideology
which works for them.

At the beginning of *Novelist Before the World,* Gironella declares:

The novelist born in Castile and desiring to interpret life in France will not come upon the truth. Nor will he convince the Castilians or the French with his words.[15]

The implicit but somewhat incoherently expressed problem stated here is the novelist's search for truth. Personal truths are rooted in the writer's life and tradition, and it is the rare artist who may renounce his background, family, religion, country and be successful at portraying a distinct and intelligible world.

For example, sometimes Adolfo and Miguel reveal qualities that render them unbelievable and artificial. *Where the Soil Was Shallow* begins at Miguel's birthplace of Darnius in the Spanish province of Catalonia and subsequently shifts its scene to Paris, Donegal (Ireland), southern France, Austria, and then returns to Darnius where it terminates. The portrayal of all events described in locales exclusive of Spain is unconvincing even though Miguel, like the author himself, knows Europe through his travels.

Gironella himself recognized this novel's amateurish qualities; he was surprised that it won the Nadal Prize.[16] The author had not learned much about writing novels after completing his first one, *Where the Soil Was Shallow,* or his second one. Integrating history with fiction in *The Tide,* Gironella created a set of German personages and situated the entire action of the novel in Germany just before and during World War II. These are unique and unbelievable stereotypes of Germans and Nazis, unquestionably deriving from the author's imagination. Obviously Gironella had never been in Germany and knew very little about German tradition. In fact, he told me that *The Tide* was a total fabrication and that he had never travelled to Germany before or during its composition.[17] He intended to synthesize as best he could a historical novel about the events of World War II. His chief interest was to reproduce the atmosphere and reality of wartime Germany.

Whatever the stylistic defects of his first two novels, both works are written with extraordinary vigor; their feeling of exhilaration and their vitality of prose may be partly explained by the novelist's anxiety for success and popularity. His first two novels probably fall into the category of popular literature.

Greater writers than Gironella began their careers and evolved as artists after serving similar literary apprenticeships. In fact, critics usually compare him to Charles Dickens, as does Anthony Kerrigan: ". . . it is Dickens that he resembles in method, prejudice and intent."[18]

By 1953, the year in which *The Cypresses Believe in God* was published, Gironella had become prominent in Spain. His insistence on writing in this novel about things Spanish, combined with the prolonged and voluminous character of the novel and its inventory of human types and the Spanish spirit, is an accurate implementation of the goals partially described in *Novelist* and subsequently attained in *The Cypresses*. Although Gironella did not rely upon *Novelist Before the World* entirely for the creation of *The Cypresses* since his ideas about the novel and his career were constantly changing, he was convinced that in *Novelist* he had laid the cornerstone of his literary career and had found a formula for continued success. His early novels, however amateurish they were, display certain aspects of Gironella's aesthetic doctrines which matured with later literary successes such as *The Cypresses Believe in God*. *Novelist Before the World*, then, is not only an index to his early works but probably plays a formative role in the writer's subsequent career. *Novelist* should be considered as a list of partially fulfilled concepts deriving from a glowing, youthful idealism and pertaining particularly to the author's first two published novels. At the same time, his is a doctrine of aspirations whose goals a lifetime may never fulfill.

Novelist contains much in microcosmic form guiding Gironella's development and maturation. For example, when he had proposed that the Spanish novelist adjust his perspectives to include the international scene, he foreshadowed his debut into travel books and essays. Again, paradoxically, his greatest literary successes have been novels based upon his attempts to clarify Spain's internal political entanglements before and during the Civil War. Gironella believes that *The Cypresses Believe in God* and its sequel, *One Million Dead*, escaped condemnation because in 1953 Spain anticipated entering the European Common Market. General Franco had suspended restrictions on certain cultural activities, preferring to project a liberal image. Recognizing the great obstacle that lay in censorship, Gironella indirectly became a leader against it. Publishing two novels and several essays directly related to the Civil War was a courageous step. Even so, it is evident that Gironella began his literary career cautiously, writing about themes that would not offend the Franco regime. Similarly, his *Novelist Before the World* is an equally cautious, somewhat eclectic, and at times a tautological volume—a fairly accurate reflection of his early career.

CHAPTER 2

Major Themes

JOSÉ María Gironella selected eight major themes or topics about which to construct his novels and also his essays: Romantic heroes and heroines, the Civil War, life and death, religion, travel, politics, his work and himself. Gironella limits himself to these themes and his well-established stylistic approach for literary success. Thus, he revived nineteenth-century concepts of Realism, preferring to create for his own time a kind of Gironellan *comédie humaine*. His early novels, *Where the Soil Was Shallow* and *The Tide*, share the major interests of Spain's nineteenth-century writers thematically and seem true anachronisms.

I *The Romantic Hero*

Gironella's early heroes and heroines emerge from the Romantic frame of reference of Chateaubriand and his *mal du siècle* but with protagonists considerably updated to include some late nineteenth and early twentieth century characteristics of Realist writers.

Nevertheless, the Gironellan hero of his first novel, *Where the Soil Was Shallow*, cannot be compared to the heroine of his latest novel, *Woman, Arise and Walk*. Miguel Serra of *Where the Soil Was Shallow*, the author's first romantic hero with realist qualities, is the first step in Gironella's departure from the nineteenth century and Romanticism. Successive novels show a transformation from Romantic-Realism to the contemporary modern hero or heroine as is especially evidenced by Myriam of *Woman*.

In his early novels, the author's heroes and heroines exemplify the classic-romantic archetype and his extreme egotism, erratic nature, and exaggerated actions. The heroes and heroines of his later fictional works renounce the "Romantic pose" for contemporary attitudes of inner-directedness, societal alienation and possible mental aberration. Although for his early romanticized character creations, love was the best resolution to difficulties, his later creations may speak of love but regard the concept as unfathomable and almost meaningless. Nevertheless, all the author's heroes and heroines are subject to one particular catalyst: Gironella's personal conception of reality. What may have begun with the creation of a flatly stereotyped romantic character in his early novels matures to a closely detailed imitation and projection of the character's complex contemporaries.

II *The Civil War*

War is always a stimulating subject for the novelist because of its exciting events and their consequences. Fortunately for his readers, José María Gironella lived through those eventful Civil War years in Spain where he fought as a youth for the Falange. It is unfortunate that Gironella did not describe and document adequately his own experiences during these years and his Civil War novels lack this immediacy in situations he describes. Still, they are far more ambitious projects than a collection of reminiscences would be. Their approach reveals the impact of war realistically upon characters and families like those of the *romans à fleuve* (Generation novels) of the nineteenth century. His first-hand sources assure historical accuracy and completeness of detail of the events described, for Gironella owns a large collection of photographs and newspapers from which he worked to document *The Cypresses Believe in God*, the novel that describes the period 1931-36. He considers these documents and his own war experiences essential to explain the politics of those years. Considering these as primary sources, Gironella is unconcerned by the fictional works of other members of his generation such as Max Aub, Arturo Barea or Ramón Sender, who have already published their own intensely personal and semifictional versions of the same events. Furthermore, Gironella does not care to read the accounts of any writer that might disturb or confuse his own vision of truth.[1] Great attention to historical accuracy and detail

and concern for the actions of his protagonists combine to raise
the question as to whether Gironella is novelist, historian, or a
combination of both. He regards both as essential. Self-taught,
Gironella's first exposure to literature that combined elements
both of history and fiction were the *Episodios nacionales* (*National
Episodes*) of Benito Pérez Galdós. He acknowledges Galdós as
his first teacher: "Galdós taught me what not to do!"[2] For Gironella, however, Galdós' error was that he did not integrate history
with fiction and treats them as separate and distinct in his
Episodes. Correcting Galdós' "misconception," Gironella feels he
fuses historical events with fiction for greater truth in action.
Thus, he feels he obtains emotionally dramatic elements within
the historical frame, which endow them with the "splendor of
truth."

With this personal and literary aesthetic in mind, Gironella
wrote *The Cypresses Believe in God* where his Alvear family of
Gerona typically represents all Spanish families between 1931 and
1936. The novel's hero, Ignacio, is a fictional projection of himself
and the novel gains in authenticity since the novel contains many
biographical elements.[3] Consequently, *The Cypresses* is an excellent example of the writer's attempt to fuse history with fiction
in evidence of the author's need for self-expression.

Its sequel, *One Million Dead*, has less emotional impact than
its predecessor. Possibly the period 1936-39 had fewer events to
fit into the author's "fusion" formula. Nor do the fictionalized
personal dramas of the Alvear family satisfy the author's narrative purpose here. Although occasional descriptive sections of
the novel breathe life into the politicians, warmongers, and
townspeople that form the real and artistic material for his portrait of the Civil War years, *One Million Dead* emerges as historical reportage rather than as a historical novel. Gironella does
not quite implement his ideal of fusion. He so delights in documentation that he forsakes the Alvear family's fictional problems
for several chapters of sheer history. Thus, his sustained documentation annoys readers chiefly interested in revelation of
character and plot. In fact, Gironella is a historian who utilizes
fiction to give vent to his serious political concerns and prefers
reading works of Political Science and scientific tracts rather
than fiction.[4] Historian or novelist, his choice to write about the
Civil War emerges from his own past and his interest in it.

III   *Life and Death Dualism*

Nearly every important writer treats of the meaning of life and the role of death within life. For the Spanish spirit, this life-death dualism is usually linked with Catholicism. Unlike other Spanish writers, Gironella relegates the Catholic vision of death and the hereafter to a minor position and replaces it by his own cosmology and his own personal universe. The life-death theme has exerted tremendous force upon him: it affects his perception, his vitality, his creativity. Since this theme is basic to Spanish life and literature, the author could not have made a more popular choice than to follow his Civil War novels with a series of short stories about life and death.

Gironella considers death as an aesthetic experience to be integrated into his writing. His experience of being near death has caused him to view death both realistically and surrealistically. His realistic view is based on his personal preoccupation with the inevitable and how he intends to meet it. This shows clearly in his autobiographical work, *Los fantasmas de mi cerebro* (*Phantoms of My Brain*). His nervous breakdown brought him to the brink of death and the author describes his incoherent speculations on the nature of life, death, the universe, and himself. *Phantoms* is Gironella's attempt to reevaluate the meaning of health, his physical-mental condition and the significance of happiness.

However, death viewed surrealistically has been a more creative and rewarding experience. Gironella immerses himself totally in the subject and attacks it with the perception newly acquired as a direct result of his illness. He describes the variety of forms which death assumes as a creative stimulus. Thus, the first section of *Todos somos fugitivos* (*We Are All Fugitives*) consists of a collection of unique and highly stylized narratives which examine the psychological and philosophical standpoints of the death motif and marks the writer's entry into an entirely new literary genre—the short story. *Phantoms* and *Fugitives* are distinct stylistically and difficult to assess, but the life-death dualism is the outstanding and dominant thematic element common to both works. *Phantoms* presents Gironella's state of mind at the peak of pessimism and suicidal tendencies but *Fugitives* restores his optimism, confidence, and artistry. It accentuates the positive

values of his nervous breakdown and illustrates a new burst of
spiritual and creative vitality. Obviously, the author's nervous
breakdown was the turning point in his life and career. It renewed and deepened his faith in life as it also developed his
gnawing skepticism, his lack of trust, and his greater artistic
concern for life's meaning.

IV   Religious Concepts

José María Gironella is a Catholic who wavers in his commitment to his faith. Most of his literary works contain skeptics as
well as some who accept Catholicism totally. Belief in God is
one of Gironella's greatest problems. This preoccupation is
shared by many Catholics in Spain where more than ninety-nine
per cent of the population profess Catholicism although many
may not practice it. The Civil War, philosophical and intellectual
crises, in short, a myriad of reasons may cause a Spaniard to
forsake Catholicism temporarily only to return. If this is or is
not Gironella's pattern, it remains a persistent suggestion in his
life and work. The author exploits his religious doubts artistically
since many of his Spanish Catholics display religious uncertain-
ties in a Gironellan-created work just as do English Catholics in
a Graham Greene novel. If we presume that the heroes and
heroines of his novels project the author's own religious beliefs,
those with whom Gironella identifies himself, it appears that a
continual recession towards an increasingly skeptical view is
evident and that his most contemporary character creations are
his most irreligious. When asked whether or not he is a practicing
Catholic, Gironella declared that he is an "enlightened one."[5]

In *The Cypresses*, César Alvear's complete faith in God, his
total commitment to the Catholic Church could never be shared
by his brother Ignacio since the latter is an intellectual trusting
to education through life's experiences rather than the mystical
appeal of the Church. For Ignacio, Catholicism may offer certain
solutions to various problems in life but it cannot resolve his
own problems. In his early work, *La marea* (*The Tide*), the
religious theme does not occupy a key position unless the condemnation of Nazi fanaticism be considered as the author's
commentary on any religious or political group carrying the
power of faith to extremes.

In a recent novel, *Woman, Arise and Walk,* Myriam is Gironella's best example of a personality totally systemless, irreligious,
and not particularly Spanish. His works are, therefore, moral
but not necessarily Catholic. Gironella has not yet written the
great Catholic novel in Spain, nor does he intend to do so. In
fact, as a result of his later skepticism, he has suggested a return
according to his idea of a Christian ethical code but not a renewal of Catholic religious principles. Gironella does not imagine
himself to be a prophet but a Christian moralist like Galdós. In
addition, he is impressed by the decor of Catholicism—its inspirational force, its architecture, even by its odors. He separates
Church doctrine from ecclesiástical aesthetics.

As a youth in Spain, Gironella read and learned Catholic
dogmas as a prospective priest. The interruption of civil war
shook his vocation and caused areas of doubt so that he found
it necessary to test, accept, or reject particular Catholic principles. This did not mean he rejected his Catholic heritage and
he has been always fond of describing clerical types[6] and
ecclesiastical mechanics. His later skepticism, however, is not a
natural outgrowth of this early development but derives from a
conscientious effort towards self-enlightenment brought on by
the perplexity of Civil War politics and its repercussions. Although Gironella has never offered an explanation of the source
of his doubts, he implies that his personal ethic is an outgrowth
of his belief in God, Catholicism, and his doubts. Moreover,
key works which directly or indirectly establish the author's
religious position—the Civil War novels and his recent work,
Woman, Arise and Walk—present contrasting religious perspectives and a gradual change of ideology between 1953 and 1962.

V *International Perspectives*

As a journalist in the early 1940's, Gironella observed and
reported the essentials of current newsworthy events, and the
author's experience sharpened his perceptions. His perspectives
widened when he began his travels outside Spain, not only
strengthening him as a foreign correspondent but adding a
proper distance from which he might survey Spain and its relationship to the world. Such articles reflect only minor "peninsular" subjects and not until his nervous breakdown did a

necessity for change of scene affect him deeply. While seeking medical aid for his "biological disorder" in Helsinki, Vienna, Copenhagen, and Paris, documentation of his travels for a series of travel books of his "foreign experiences" as seen through the eyes of a Spanish tourist appealed to him. When most Spaniards were too engrossed in daily problems to look beyond their national frontiers, with ideological infiltration restricted to a minimum as a result of Franco's censorship in the early 1950's, Gironella initiated his "travelogues" with the publication of *Viaje en torno a la revolución cubana* (*Journey into the Cuban Revolution*) in Barcelona's *Gaceta ilustrada* (*Illustrated Gazette*), describing a first-hand account of Fidel Castro's government during its early days. His travelogues were written with facility and integrity and since international reporting in Spain was rare, the majority of news items is published through Reuters or United Press and allows for little interpretation.

His next publications, *Persons, Ideas and Seas* and *Japan and Her Ghosts*, are transitional and reflect an indecision of choice between a personal and objective note or a compromise between the two points. They demonstrate Gironella's conflict of interests only resolved in his latest work, *China, lágrima innumerable* (*China, Countless Tears*). Even today Gironella associates his work closely with the demands of public taste, and continues to write travelogues.

VI *Politics*

Gironella's vital and vitriolic point of view forced him to seek a non-political expression of his keen critical ability and historical sense. He chose China and Cuba, centers of world Communism, and directed his arguments against them. His political opinions suggest that he is an educator, a demagogue, possibly a politician in Spain after Franco's death. Although his political motives are unclear, many Spanish writers before him have made such a successful transition. He writes as a man of the people, firm in his opinions, expounding them with an appearance of freedom. In Franco's Spain, his writings on Communism have met with public approval. A Catholic historian in the United States has translated his political essays fairly recently.[7]

VII *Autocriticism*

Gironella occasionally contributes auto-critical articles to enhance his work and thereby fills gaps with accurate information concerning the genesis of a particular work or points in his biography. Occasionally an article appears that attempts to appraise his ability. For example, his essays on the genesis of *The Cypresses Believe in God* and its sequel, *One Million Dead*, give straightforward accounts of his *modus operandi*. Gironella's autocritical articles have helped to corroborate debatable points and clarify biographical data.

VIII *Autobiography*

José María Gironella writes about himself in characters projecting his experiences but he usually subordinates autobiography to his fictional purpose. In his early days, he struggled to create characters and personages that were true personalities. Unfortunately, Miguel Serra and Adolfo Stolberg were vapid stereotypes with whom he sought personal identification through a series of unreal experiences. Realizing that his personal life was more valid, Gironella abandoned fiction as a mask and defense mechanism to describe himself and his thoughts artistically under the *guise* of fiction. The success of *The Cypresses* strengthened this development and he cast off the limitation of fiction altogether, committing his private feelings to print. *Phantoms of My Brain*, written after his nervous breakdown, concerns himself and his illness.

Gironella's books become increasingly personal and evidence a new artistic vision. After personal intimacy, revelation of the external world about him in personal terms affords a prism through which reality filters to emerge more vividly than before. The superficial, cautious disciple of Spain's nineteenth-century writers had etched a new public image for himself, attaining recognition from his public and a degree of personal security as well. Gironella now prefers to express personal idiosyncracies through his books on travel, world politics and history, and emerges an expansive and overpowering personality.

CHAPTER 3

A Romantic World

I Gironella's First Romantic-Realist Hero

THE most important theme in Gironella's early novels is his description of man—man in search of himself in the labyrinth of society. His first novel, *Un hombre* (*Where the Soil Was Shallow*), is an autobigraphical and romantic work.[1] The settings of the novel include Donegal, San Sebastian, Darnius, Paris, Rennes, Munich, and Budapest. However, most of the action crucial to the development of the protagonist, Miguel Serra, takes place in Donegal, Ireland.

Miguel and his mother Eva are the chief personages. His father, Antonio, never appears in the novel but is referred to occasionally to explain his influence on Miguel's life. A native of Darnius, Antonio was a contrabass player proud of his Catalan heritage but a wanderer always. After Gironella succinctly narrates the courtship of Antonio and Eva in flashback, we discover that Eva's strong sexual attraction for Antonio diminishes in the early years of their marriage and that a spiritual gap, not originally recognized, separates them. Shortly after Miguel's birth, Antonio dies and Eva is left alone to rear and educate her son. The principal theme of the novel is Miguel's growth. Through experience and self-analysis, Miguel searches for a suitable career and meaning for his life.

Miguel encounters scores of minor personages in his spiritual quest. They are utilized effectively to reflect his growth throughout the narrative. Nolan, his mother's business manager, exercises the role of substitute father and disciplinarian. Each of Miguel's women occupies a particular place in his struggle to understand other human hearts. Isabel, daughter of a neighboring farmer, is his constant companion during early youth with whom he first experiences "adolescent" love. Later, Jeannette, whom Miguel meets in the south of France, fulfills his ideal of "romantic" love —passionate, transitory, futile. Finally Yvonne, Miguel's mistress in Paris, achieves the closest and most intimate sexual relationship with him. However, when Miguel becomes a circus impresario, dozens of minor characters are included in the narrative, briefly but accurately sketched. Miguel plays a variety of roles himself—seminarist, book seller, university student, circus manager, dandy. The novel depicts Miguel's failure in each new career.

Where the Soil Was Shallow epitomizes the author's crises, vacillations, discouragements, failures. As a liberal arts student in Dublin, Miguel is frustrated by the vacuity of his studies and is dropped from the rolls. The sudden and accidental death of his mother distracts him further. He loses interest in his bookstore after deliberately seeking security in this sound enterprise as suggested by Nolan, his mother's financial adviser. When he considers marriage with Jeannette, a leading trapeze artist, he is rejected and, not quite understanding his destiny, he remains on the periphery of society, a restless, rootless and sensitive personality—a potential artist.

One of the most sincere revelations of personality occurs as the novel ends. Miguel achieves total communication with Ruben, an ex-employee of Miguel's ill-fated circus. Both decide to return to Darnius after a series of "picaresque" adventures. Lacking discipline and worn out by his professional and amorous failures, Miguel returns to Darnius to lead a perfunctory existence in a society completely alien to his cosmopolitan background and development. The plot of *Where the Soil Was Shallow* is surprisingly simple for it only traces the activities, growth and education of a young man.

A basic problem with the novel is that the reader knows from the outset, Miguel will not triumph, for his search for ideal values is hopeless from the very beginning. Although his greatest strength is his freedom to choose his destiny, Miguel has the financial security to afford this search but lacks character and vitality to achieve his purposes. Stylistic contrast between "colorful" events and the "grayness" of Miguel's personality is clearly defined and demonstrates the lack of harmony between Miguel's spiritual life and the society in which he lives. As the novel opens, Miguel is spiritually empty. At the conclusion, he is equally vacuous. Miguel's chief problem is his inability to particularize serious goals while proceeding on his spiritual journey.

The delineation of Miguel's character loses in intensity when the author inserts a multitude of episodic incidents that detract from his protagonist's development. However, the sections in which Gironella explores Miguel's relationship with his mother are the most significant in the entire novel for they reflect the writer's attempt to reveal personal experience. Miguel's upbringing, like Gironella's, commands our interest, not because it is unusual in any sense but because the story of a young man's maturity helps us better to appreciate lives and to perceive problems. James Joyce, F. Scott Fitzgerald, and Thomas Wolfe, among others, have documented their childhood experiences at least semiautobiographically, while writing novels of situations encountered in their particular milieus. Gironella, however, followed their example only to a point. Although skeletal autobiographical facts are partially adhered to, the chief difficulty with *Where the Soil Was Shallow* is its falsification of the worlds in which the author did *not* live. Despite autobiographical similarities, Gironella is detached from what he describes. Consequently, the novel suffers from artificiality whose episodic incident replaces badly needed sections explaining motivations and inner feelings. When Miguel begins his spiritual search, we try to understand his motives. However, his experiences represent confusions and departures from the real issues of the novelist—the anarchic spirit in his protagonist and in himself. Thus, if we view Miguel's failures as attempts to make concrete his goals, only then do these hazily sketched vignettes impart greater philosophical meaning. Of course, careful integration, explanation, and execution of the events themselves in the novelist's personal life would have resulted in a greater artistic achievement for Gironella. A first novel, *Where the Soil Was Shallow* shows the author's lack of concentration successfully to come to grips with the revelation of character. Therefore, it is a somewhat superficial and melodramatic work. Still, the upshot of its success in Spain and its winning of the Nadal Prize can best be explained in this commentary:

What appears more certain is that Gironella urges his generation to seek truth, shun an aimless and driftless existence, and take a positive stand on the issues of life.[2]

Historically, Miguel's spiritual search is the author's own quest for a new life after the shattering experiences of the Civil War. Although Gironella carefully avoids presenting this motivation as the chief impetus, he substitutes Miguel's mother's death as the principal reason for his spiritual quest. Her death symbolizes the end of a matriarchy—Spain cast into upheaval because of civil war. Just as many Spaniards were forced to cut the umbilical cord and search for a new value system, Miguel's spiritual journey is symbolic of all Spaniards' search for new directions after the chaos of war. Gironella uses Eva's death to explain symbolically what cannot be published directly because of the rigors of Franco's censorship.

II *Continuing Romantic-Realism*

Gironella's second novel, *La marea* (*The Tide*), received little recognition despite the writer's obvious improvement in style and technique. What *Where the Soil Was Shallow* lacked in organization and balance because of a young writer's inexperience and exuberance, *The Tide* made up for in professional skill. Gironella had learned from past errors. *The Tide* presents a cohesive plot in a highly realistic historical setting. Events themselves help to determine the fictional lives of the personages. However, its plot is melodramatic rather than imaginative although *The Tide* extends Gironella's search further into man and his problems.

The author has chosen Southern Germany during the period 1933-38 or the rise of Naziism for the action of the novel. As the title suggests, *The Tide* is the tide of Naziism that will rise and sweep Germany either to glory or to defeat, where no one must resist or question the moral posture of the New Order. Adolfo Stolberg, a dedicated architect, model of physical and mental health, adventurous, ideal incarnate of the German Youth Movement, is caught up in the surge of Naziism. In the summer of 1938, Adolfo spends his vacation at a famous health resort in Baden and meets his future wife, Enna Stragg. Enna is twenty-two, a blonde worshipper of nature, the perfect female specimen according to the philosophical principles of the Nazi movement. Both are egoists and mutually appreciative of the other's physical attributes. Despite Enna's constant companionship with Eduardo (who later dies in battle for the glory of the Third Reich), a tragic occurrence brings Enna and Adolfo together—the suicide of Enna's friend, Olga. Just as Michelangelo Antonioni, the famous Italian film director, shifts the narrative focus in his film *L'avventura* (*The Adventure*), so Gironella controlled his narrative of *The Tide*. Olga's death occurs early in the novel and accelerates the intellectual and physical relationship between Adolfo and Enna although it has no other function in the plot. Gironella implies even greater significance. It symbolizes a philosophy founded upon vanity and perverted idealism. In this context, Enna and Adolfo begin their relationship. Olga, a moody, intense, introspective girl, is incapable of adapting herself to the specifications of the New Order. Her reasons for suicide remain a mystery although they are linked to feelings of inferiority. Her tragedy gives Enna an opportunity with Adolfo. Their romantic correspondence finally ends in the couple's marriage.

Another pair, Gustavo and Wanda, in their love compare and contrast with the romance of Adolfo and Enna. Gustavo is Adolfo's brother, individualist in his convictions, poetic in his expression. Wanda is his Polish-refugee sweetheart. A sensitive and talented musician, she practices the organ in empty churches. While Adolfo and Enna sacrifice themselves totally to the demands of Naziism, Gustavo and Wanda stand firm, preserving their artistry and integrity even though it cost them their lives. Both Stolberg brothers seek truth in their respective professions and amorous relationships but Gustavo triumphs and survives the impact of Nazi ideological indoctrinations because he is essentially flexible, adaptable, a realist who reconciles himself to any geographical area or philosophy.

German military stereotypes are scattered throughout the novel, the most important of whom is General Von Mansfield, in charge of espionage. He is the third man and eventually destroys Adolfo's marriage. He is also instrumental in using Wanda as a guinea pig for Nazi "human experimentation." The novel slowly traces the disintegration of the perfect "biological union" of Adolfo and Enna as well as that of the Nazi ideals, already undermining a formerly "healthy" society.

In accordance with the tenets of racial superiority, Enna decides to "breed" a child sired by Von Mansfield. At this point, Adolfo, aware of his wife's indiscretions and the progressive decay of German society, asserts himself. He begins to work against Naziism and suffers an emotional collapse analogous to Germany's military defeat. With neither love of his wife nor integrity of his career, Adolfo commits suicide. Enna also dies in an air raid on her way to a meeting with Von Mansfield who has already discarded her and the "genetic experiment" for another voluptuous blonde. Wanda meets her fate early in the novel at the hands of Enna's father, Doctor Stragg, a fiendish scientific experimenter. Gustavo escapes to Scandinavia with his ideals intact.

The greatest asset of this novel is its depiction of an entire world, unified and integrated in the historical period it describes with personages and problems well developed in a realm of possibility. Even Adolfo's unpredictable suicide is credible because of the accurate presentation of his feelings and the motives which led to this act. The novel's action moves at a rapid, nervous pace to its conclusion and its emotional rhythm is like the long sweep of a giant wave that gains impetus, crashes on the shore, and recedes slowly back to sea. In contrast to *Where the Soil Was Shallow, The Tide* is a tense, highly organized, and far better written novel. Its unity results from its surprising economy and deftness. For all of these good qualities, *The Tide* fails because of Gironella's limited perspective. No matter how logically conceived or easily visualized, his personages are stereotypes and colorless creatures representing a concept rather than vital incarnations of reality. Despite excellent delineation, they are used as props. If the author's intention was to render the Nazi movement and its effects upon Germany dramatically with no other purpose but to entertain, he has succeeded only in writing a commercial best seller. Because of its emphasis on dialogue and extremely visual prose effects, it could be adapted into a scenario for a grade-B war film. Thus, the presentation of Enna's death demonstrates Gironella's ability to write graphic prose:

The bombs kept on falling. She saw their glow in the air and heard the sound of gunfire.... "Hurrah! Hurrah! Another one destroyed!" And why had she fallen on the ground into a trench? "It's better to be on your feet to see the battle," she thought. "Okay, perhaps it's better to be on the ground. Oh!"

There was a stain on the grass, a red stain. Her clothing, her entire stomach was soaked in blood. It must have been a hemorrhage, but with all the bombs and her tiredness, she didn't know what happened to her.[3]

Obviously, Gironella gave his career definition by describing themes not attempted by other Spanish authors. He had little choice for he could not write about Spain and the Civil War at this time.

III   Comparison of Romantic Heroes of Early Novels

The salient feature that redeems these early novels is their portrayal of the "romantic life" of their protagonists. In fact, Romantic elements pervade subsequent novels as well. His early novels, in particular, show the gradual transformation of his Romantic protagonists into complex modern figures typical of the twentieth century. Gironella characterizes the Romantic life by liberal attitudes, visionary thoughts, egotism, exciting emotions and strong reliance on the imagination and sentiment, some elements which these protagonists share. For example, in *Where the Soil Was Shallow* Gironella created a hero reminiscent of Pío Baroja's *Zalacaín el aventurero* (*Zalacaín the Adventurer*), egocentric, erratic, but endowing the novel with a true vitality. Miguel Serra shows the energies of a sensitive youth asking fundamental questions, reacting egotistically and emotionally, seeking answers from an unresponsive world. Gironella defines Miguel's nature in the following commentary: "... fanciful, cunning, inconsistent, the qualities of a man who has given up and who is hardhearted."[4] Jacques Barzun's remarks as to the nature of "romantic life" applies to Gironella's early personages:

Romantic striving may be summed up as the effort to create order out of experience individually acquired. It is a striving because human experience does not automatically dictate its own forms or point out its own values. That the task of a man is to discover these for himself is shown by his possession of energies and desires.[5]

Miguel's life centers about his goals of making existence stable and of providing it with stability through attaining feasible goals. Of course, his chief difficulty is to ascertain which goals are feasible. "He was intelligent, although a bit shy, with a complex and anarchic sensitivity. He rebelled intimately against the drivel of his youth."[6] Another interesting romantic element is Miguel's communion with nature:

Physical empathy with nature was typical for Miguel. Before nightfall, his sense of hearing was sharpened, his sense of smell unlocked; his eyes insisted on piercing the darkness and the tips of his fingers violently perceived the coldness of the balcony's railing or any object. In the evening his major illusion was to contemplate the heavens with some powerful telescope.[7]

Unlike archromantics, Miguel also considered himself a Realist, individualist and materialist in the twentieth-century mode. He is a skeptic who, like his mother, continually doubts. He is, consequently, rebellious, unable to accept his limitations as seminary student, collegian, lover, bookseller and circus impresario. Refusing to commit himself, Miguel resigns himself to a peripheral position in his society and to the pseudoromantic pose of the contemplative intellectual, the *señorito* (master of the house) living alone from his inheritance.

Miguel is dependent on no one for love or inspiration. After his mother's death, he is totally alone in the world. He sobs only once, and this is his single emotional display in the entire novel. Where a romantic figure fulfilled in love should be at his best, Miguel displays the sangfroid of a restrained, excessively ego-oriented personality. His relationship with Yvonne, his mistress, is strictly unilateral—she gives, he takes. Much later in the novel, his affair with Jeannette represents the fulfillment of a romantic idea begun at their meeting years earlier on the road to Rennes. But when Miguel asks Jeannette's hand in marriage, she refuses, preferring her freedom. Miguel is left with no other recourse but to recognize that his destiny is to remain alone.

As a university student, Miguel states a number of principles that reveal the transformation of his romantic nature:

Life lacks meaning except for the religious man, the artist and the primitive. Not even these exceptions are valid since the religious man doesn't aspire to happiness but to death. The artist constantly suffers in order to create and the primitive man is not capable of understanding his privileged situation. [. . .] Intellectuals are the most unfortunate beings of the universe since they want most to be gods. Love is no solution either since each sex demands that the other provide happiness and instead, they create a wasteland. Even the goodness of nature is a myth. The bodies of ninety percent of women are horrible. Satisfaction of our instincts leads to pain. It's stupid to despair since there is nothing better. What matters is just to go on living.[8]

Miguel confirms his materialistic values, his condemnation of
naïveté and sentimentalism, his disenchantment with the romantic life of those relying on nature for inspiration, women, and
sexual love for fulfillment and suffering.

To profess such a philosophy and to adhere to it is quite
another matter. Although Miguel argues against Romantic ideals,
he does not succeed in convincing us of total adherence to his
principles because of the ambiguity of his acts. Gironella may
have created these ambiguities because of his own lack of conviction, artistic instability, and inexperience as a writer. Yet
Miguel is still a Gironellan hero, partially a child of the Romantic-
Realist era coming of age rapidly in the twentieth century. In
fact, he evolves into more of a contemporary personage than
Gironella probably designed, and resembles his author more
than Gironella himself had intended.

In his second novel, *The Tide*, Adolfo Stolberg represents a
further transformation of Gironella's idea of a romantic figure
and is described more realistically: "An architect, a conservative,
in the classical mold."[9] The antithesis of Miguel Serra, he lacks a
sensitive nature. Adolfo is austere and represents the iron-willed,
career-minded, talented German at midpoint between Romanticism and Realism. At one extreme, his brother Gustavo represents Romanticism and his wife Enna symbolizes the progressive,
patriotic, anarchic type of Romantic-Realism evolving from
Naziism. Gustavo Stolberg is a poet, an idealist. He is Gironella's
porte-parole and expresses the lyrical side of the Stolberg family
spirit—one open to Adolfo were he not committed to building
monuments to the glory of the Third Reich. Enna represents
Gironella's personal disgust at the perversion of the German
Romantic ideal. However, Adolfo's predicaments interest us most.

Adolfo is a naïve and ineffectual lover. His Romantic marriage
proposal would be extremely humorous without his naïveté:

I love you, Enna. You'll be more beautiful even after your youth is
past. You'll help me to be the best architect in the country. Come and
live with me. I'll always treat you like a gentleman . . .[10]

Yet Adolfo's attitude is explained by his worship of German
scientism and what is concrete and functional. Work is Adolfo's
life and the resolution to his problems. When Enna and Adolfo
fall out of love, he clings to the idea of building an entire city,

an ideal which helps him to meet the crisis of his marriage. Both
Adolfo and Serra have a realistic view of death, although Adolfo
is more dispassionate and possesses a stronger will to cope with
death. Yet, realizing he has nothing left to live for because of
his wife's infidelity and the total decadence of Germany, Adolfo
takes poison, a deliberately romantic and tragic suicide. With
Enna gone, he has neither inspiration nor future.

Without the vigor and imagination of a romantic hero, Adolfo
displays passion when he beats his wife for infidelity. Otherwise,
he is less and less a romantic figure, perhaps because Gironella
altered his original romantic conception. What begins as a love
story between two young Germans before the Second World
War ends as a melodramatic medley of improbable incident and
serious attempts to provide historical accuracy. His Romantic
figures became subservient to the demands of a more complex
and highly mechanized modern society.

IV   The "Modern" Gironellan Hero

In his Civil War novels, Ignacio Alvear is closer to our conception of the modern Gironellan hero. Ignacio represents a
synthesis of the qualities already described in his predecessors
and demonstrates the transformation from the Romantic-Realist
figure to a modern hero with Romantic qualities. He is as erratic
as Miguel Serra during his youth. In fact, Ignacio's early years
parallel both Miguel's and the author's biography. In *One Million
Dead*, Ignacio shows the same rational qualities proving detrimental to Adolfo in *The Tide*. His perspective is less romantic
because Gironella is growing more interested in history than in
character.

However, in *The Cypresses Believe in God*, Ignacio, a sensitive youth reared by a pious family in a religion in which he no
longer believes, rejects the seminary to live in the secular world.
Unlike his brother César who idealistically embraces the Catholic faith, Ignacio becomes a pragmatist with his own Christian
principles. His ability to think and act individually makes him
a modern figure. Experience is his true test for life which commands the respect of his family who cannot understand his
actions or his intellect. Ignacio's youth and early actions reflect
the Romantic idealism and avant-garde radicalism of the Civil

War period. He has only three meaningful personal relationships in the course of two thousand pages, and each of his women is only a reflection of his growth.

In his adolescence, Ignacio meets Ana María at a resort in San Feliü de Guíxols and is impressed by her physical beauty. Romantically smitten, he considers his youthful love for Ana María an ideal. Gironella describes their first meeting:

The most important thing was to be a man, to advance, to get ahead in his career. Now he would spend the next two weeks, dreaming. . . . About love, the truth is that he understood very little. Suddenly he didn't know what had happened. A blue balloon drew near him from the sea and, boom! It seemed like his heart swelled.

Ana María could hardly breathe. Her legs remained immobile. Besides she had just realized that the pedal boat was also named Ana María, the one that Ignacio had just selected without realizing it.[11]

They spend many romantic evenings together on the Costa Brava before Ana María returns to Barcelona. Ignacio continues to write adolescent outpourings attesting to Ana María's dazzling beauty and Ignacio's own fascination. But Ignacio is in love with love and not with Ana María herself.

His second "romantic" experience is unpleasant. Ignacio contracts venereal disease from Canela, a prostitute of the main street of Gerona. His short-lived "affair" with Canela serves as Ignacio's sexual initiation into manhood and nothing more since he has little contact with her after this experience.

Against a background of political and social discontent in Catalonia, Ignacio finally meets his true love, Marta. Their idyllic relationship with the added resources of melodrama, wartime assassinations, and dangers through their Civil War experiences create a love story in the full bloom of romantic life and in a realistic, historical setting.

V   *From Romanticism to Realist-Existentialism*

Another of Gironella's fictional personages is Myriam in his novel, *Woman, Arise and Walk*. She is described in the following manner:

. . . a young expatriate, resident of Rome, outwardly abulic and tortured spiritually, she is dragged into the vortex of two eternal and sweeping forces—Christ symbolized by the psychiatrist Enmanuale and Satan in the person of the nuclear scientist Hauer.[12]

A romantically inclined heroine, spiritually disenchanted because of continual psychological crises from her sentimental attitudes, she searches for a new system of values.

Myriam is complex. She cannot cope with the gradual yet irrevocable stream of real events that impinges upon her romantic world. Yet she cannot live by her singularly anachronistic romantic ideas of life and love but must discover the causes of her alienation from society. Without nationality, family or friends, she works sporadically as an interpreter for the more fashionable hotels in Rome. Because she experiences intense periods of solitude, she attempts suicide. Gironella sums up her character in this description: "Myriam, an expatriate of middle-class origin, shell-shocked in a bombing raid came to Rome in a state of melancholy in the spring of 1962. Ultimately she had lost even more than the desire to live. She found herself (and Myriam was conscious of it) on the border of depression. Her comment was always the same: 'What's the use of going on!' "[13]

Like Eva in *Where the Soil Was Shallow* Myriam has lost her will to live. She searches for love, faith, and a resolution to her solitude. With the German scientist Hauer, she complements her amoral spirit with his adventurousness. However, her affair with Hauer casts her further into despair and death is the only solution to her solitude. She is powerless to commit suicide. Self-love and cowardice are the two important deterrents. Myriam will only do away with herself if the experience adds to her personal delight. Gironella includes a clinical reason for Myriam's suicidal attempts. A disease analogous to scarlet fever has caused deterioration of her central nervous system, and Myriam's spiritual atrophy is directly related to her *symptomata*. The clinical phase of her illness can be cured, according to her psychiatrist, Dr. Enmanuale. Myriam's mental disorder, however, can be alleviated only if she perceives her daily life realistically. She constantly lapses into the fetal position, thus indicating her need for love. She wants a meaningful life but her sentimental attitudes prevent it. In eroticism and despair, she represents Gironella's most complex fictional as well as his most modern creation. She is a neurotic woman of contemporary society.

Her plight interests Spanish readers because Myriam is a new phenomenon in contemporary Spain. Spaniards have seldom encountered a woman spiritually drifting, uncommitted to any purpose or person. In true romantic spirit, however, Myriam will be redeemed through love. Unable to reject her desire for sexual experience, Myriam adds another dimension to her definition of love: "To love was to realize the contrary; not to look for your own happiness but the happiness of others. Thus the opportunities to love have no limits precisely because human suffering is boundless."[14] She must suffer to discover the true meaning of love if love is her only redemption. Gironella adds to Myriam's concept of love a new Christian idealism. She suffers because of her pregnancy by Hauer for this. Her miscarriage and the loss of her child are factors helping to achieve the peace of mind and spirit that she desperately sought. Unlike other Gironellan heroes or heroines, Myriam shows her dependence upon psychological therapy and science. Too weak to rely upon herself, she needs psychological adjustment.

Having examined the transformation of the romantic elements in the lives of Miguel Serra, Adolfo Stolberg, Ignacio Alvear, and Myriam, a definite progression away from the late nineteenth-century Romantic-Realist towards the more complex modern contemporary figure appears. Nevertheless, these personages share a spirit of adventure and romance suggesting Gironella's predilection for romantic life with an increasing awareness of contemporary society and its problems. If he is to keep pace with society as it is, his personages must give the appearance of reality. They are, consequently, less romantic in character and conception.

CHAPTER 4

A Writer's Fulfillment:
Los cipreses creen en Dios
(The Cypresses Believe in God)

I *Analysis of Structure, Plot and Characters*

THE cycle of Civil War novels opening with *Los cipreses creen en Dios* (*The Cypresses Believe in God*) in 1953 is one of José María Gironella's best achievements. Facing new responsibilities as a social writer, Gironella retains certain romantic ideas of his first two novels but controls them for a greater social purpose—the explanation of Spain's Civil War. He prefers to analyze its historical setting within the realm of fiction. His Civil War novels indicate this, since Gironella can be properly considered a combination novelist-historian, although he claims to be only a novelist: "As I stated before, it's a question of writing a novel and not a political essay. I have taken literally thousands of liberties in order to justify this statement. In fact, what I've intended has been the creation of a novel and consequently, I manipulated all the possibilities of true events. I have reserved at all times the right to appeal to my powers of fantasy."[1] Thus, *The Cypresses* presents a careful integration of historical data combined with fiction. It's sequel, *One Million Dead,* de-emphasizes the fictional motif for historical documentation. Gironella's war novels catapulted him to fame and earned him the name of one of Spain's foremost living authors. *The Cypresses* took Spain's National Prize for Literature of 1953 and is among his best-written popular novels.

The Cypresses is Gironella's most ambitious work, as it is his largest novel in scope, breadth, and depth up to that time. The novel has been organized into five parts and covers the pre-Civil War period, April, 1931, to July, 1936. Almost all of its action takes place in Gerona in Catalonia. Its leading personages are the Alvear family who occupy a large apartment on the Ramblas directly overlooking the Ter River.

Matías Alvear is a clerk at the local telegraph office, married to Carmen Elgazu, a devout Catholic. Living in an atmosphere of mutual respect (Matías is Castilian and Carmen is Basque), they reared three children. César, intellectually gifted, is physically weak and enters the priesthood at his mother's insistence. His sister Pilar, a sequestered girl, obedient to family and church, possesses both inner strength and a power for love. Ignacio, the novel's hero, is a restless intellectual, always demanding more from the world and himself. The action in the novel comes chiefly through the family. *The Cypresses,* however is essentially Ignacio's story, the tale of his growth, of his problems and their solution.

The Cypresses has three levels. The first is the immediate fictional problems of the Alvears, their daily life, their individual dilemmas. On a larger scale, however, they are a typical microcosm representing all Spanish families who share in the making of history during the period of civil war. Gironella transcends these fictional and historical perspectives by elevating them to a universal significance. Their struggle becomes every Spanish family's struggle and the Civil War any war in which the problem of life-death is uppermost. Limiting the action to Gerona, Gironella makes this city exemplary of all Spanish cities that experienced the scourge of war. Gironella also fulfills one of his prime postulates of the successful novelist by writing about his tradition: "In Gerona's seminary, they shaved my head and provided me with black stockings. In Gerona, my parents made their home, my wife was born, one of my sisters was baptized. In the shade of its cypress trees, those persons whom I have loved definitely believe in God."[2] The author is intimately concerned with the lives and deaths of Gerona's population. Ignacio Alvear is a symbol of the war, a spokesman for the dead and the living. He is Gironella's own voice. César Alvear and his sister Pilar are autobiographical as well, since the author uses his sisters Carmen and Concepción as models.[3]

The Alvear family at home appear in short narratives which emphasize their essential qualities and distinct personalities. At the beginning of the novel, however, Gironella deliberately holds

back information about his characters, preferring a gradual
revelation. This may be Gironella's "nineteenth century megalo-
mania."[4] Two examples reveal this quality:

Matías Alvear was forty-six years old, a civil servant working for the
Telegraph Office and part of a group of "outsiders" in Gerona. He
originally came from Madrid, spent five years in Gerona and appeared
acclimated to the city.[5]
    Carmen Elgazu bore the stamp of a new arrival to Gerona. Of aver-
age height, her jet-black hair was gathered into a bun and her head
was well placed between her shoulders. Looking at her waist indicated
she had given birth to several children. Her legs were the columns
that supported her family's existence.[6]

Although Gironella adds metaphor to physical description inten-
sifying certain qualities of his personages, sometimes he is at
cross-purposes with the larger aims of the novel. Intending to
individualize his characters, instead they are types. It is as types
that they elevate the tone of the novel from personal to universal.
    Nevertheless, by short descriptions he succeeds in arousing
the reader's curiosity to follow his protagonists further. In the
Dickensian tradition of serialized fiction, a wide range of personages other than the Alvears appear. Among these are: (1) Mosén
Alberto, the family's spiritual adviser and confessor; (2) Martínez
de Soria, aristocrat and Commander of the Army; (3) Cosme
Vila, Chief of the Communist Party and employee of the Arús
Bank; (4) Mateo Santos, Chief of the Falange and sweetheart of
Pilar; (5) *El Responsable,* Chief of the FAI and henchman of
this Communist organization; (6) the Costa brothers, factory
owners and Deputies from Gerona; (7) Doctor Roselló, Director
of the Provincial Hospital. *The Cypresses* is a mammoth novel
but it is chiefly Ignacio Alvear's story.
    Ignacio's freshness of vision when he leaves the seminary
reveals him as a visionary: "How many things there are to see,
how many trees, trains, persons! How wide the horizon is!"[7] After
the seminary, he dedicates himself to experience, to life, while
his brother César, a solitary wanderer of cemeteries, is impas-
sioned by the afterlife, discovering peace among the tombs.
    Julio García, Gerona's influential Police Chief, helps Ignacio
secure a position at the Arús Bank where Ignacio decides to work
for his *Bachillerato* (final examinations) and as clerk at the bank

simultaneously. Gironella presents a description of César's rigorous life at Collell, the Roman Catholic Seminary just outside Gerona, realistically describing the hardships involved. Alternating descriptions of family members with historical events, Gironella usually returns to describe Ignacio. Influenced by Unamuno, especially the latter's concept of *caracoles humanos* (human snails) and by the complexities of Gerona's political parties, Ignacio lives apart from political entanglements but enmeshed in intellectual argument. With Julio García for spiritual and political guide, he studies for his degree under the tutelage of David and Olga Pol, Communist activists. The novel presents programs of various political factions in Spain according to Gironella's insistence on impartiality: "My main concern is for absolute impartiality in portraying the historical and political aspects. I believe it is useless to try to sweep away bits or fragments of history. Time is relentless."[8] The political aspect of *The Cypresses*, however, favors the Nationalist platform. Anthony Kerrigan offers this perspicacious commentary concerning Gironella's supposed impartiality: "Gironella is the prophet of the low-toned voice, the partisan of the enlightening dialogue, the revolutionist who works at avoiding extreme affirmations."[9]

Through colorful conversations between its citizens, Gironella describes Gerona and its institutions such as the Café el Neutral, the Telegraph Office, and the Arús Bank, the principal sources of information in Gerona from which all lies are created and disseminated. Also, Gironella's feeling for the 1930's, his descriptions of the mores such as jazz, the Orfeón, the Peña Ciclista, are remarkably evocative: "They had founded a choral society. Individual singing died and a swarm of bicycles had permeated the city. A Glee Club and a Cycling Club, two brand new institutions. . . ."[10] Gironella intersperses his feelings with each sociological documentation, noting the changing values of Gerona, the prostitution of traditional values because of modernization. His commentaries are intended as criticisms of various institutions or people. For example, his portrait of Mosén Alberto is a satirization of all church prelates.

Mosén Alberto is César Alvear's spiritual adviser and is presented as an advocate of the Catholic religion whose secular and spiritual life centers about the Diocesan Museum. A curator, he collects religious artifacts and classifies stones and other "de-

tails" for the greater glory of God. Gironella affirms his goodness
and inner strength but criticizes Mosén Alberto because of his
"minor" commitment to life as curator. Gironella gives vent to
anticlerical feelings about Catholic intellectuals. After publication of *The Cypresses Believe in God,* Gironella declared that he
was not popular with the clergy in Gerona.[11] He touches briefly
on this serious theme, preferring to concentrate on a blend of
major and minor semifictionalized events in the lives of the
Alvear family with such examples as the family's reaction to
César's first shave. Gironella increases its importance by invest-
ing the scene with spiritual significance: "The moment he began
[to shave], someone invisible appeared to him, someone who was
at his side, who guided his hand."[12] Such minor incidents of
family life are insignificant and incidental to Gironella's serious
purpose—the portrayal of the politics and events of the Civil War
to which he continually returns to describe events and people
for a "semblance" of history and reality. Such political parties
and platforms as the CEDA, UGT, FAI, CNT, etc., demonstrate
the political prewar muddle of Spain. The Catalan Separatist
Movement, however, is discussed by Julio García and Ignacio
with little conviction or conclusion. Nevertheless, all political
events of any consequence are carefully reported and conclusions
are drawn relevant only to the Alvear family.

Gironella develops the novel chronologically, integrating character and plot with exterior political events as reported in the
newspapers of Gerona. The threat of Civil War looms for many
chapters but does not involve the protagonists until Ignacio's
cousin, José Alvear, arrives from Madrid, displaying a political
precociousness, anticlerical attitudes, and an awareness of the
impending struggle. José is Ignacio's chief source of political and
social enlightenment and he realizes his lack of "worldliness" in
José's company. Before José's arrival from Madrid, Ignacio had
never known a woman socially or sexually until an encounter
with a prostitute. "At that time, José showed him that he knew
something about life."[13] Because of José's influence, Ignacio par-
ticipates actively in politics, attending meetings of the multitude
of political parties in Gerona. Gironella describes Ignacio's excitement at his first rally as well as the fresh spirit of Spaniards
engaged in controversy. Ignacio's anarchic spirit grows as he is
caught in a dangerous cross fire. He realizes he must abandon

his newly-discovered romantic and anarchic attitude or leave Spain. He chooses to remain with his family.

José Alvear becomes Gironella's *porte-parole* for the Falange. At this point in the novel, the Second Republic has failed and general turmoil prevails in Spain. Strikes paralyze the nation and total anarchy reigns in Gerona except for unity in the Falange Party. Through José's influence, Ignacio estranges himself ideologically from his family, fails his examinations because of his new and overwhelming interest in politics. Failure and frustration, however, provide him with the necessary impetus to resume his studies with renewed vigor. With Ignacio reading Dostoevski's *Crime and Punishment*, the narrative again turns to the other Alvear children.

Gironella depicts their transition from childhood to maturity. Describing Pilar and Ignacio as they mature as part of the continual movement of life, Gironella writes the following passages: "She let down her braids and passed her hands through her hair, carressing it. . . . Yes, she was already a woman."[14] "Just trim the sideburns and shave my neck."[15] As Ignacio spoke the preceding words to his barber, Pilar looked into her mirror at her long hair and finely proportioned body. One of Gironella's stylistic virtues is his statment of simple truths revealing universal yet intimate experiences with a minimum of emphasis. In describing women, however, he falters. (His wife Magda reads those sections in his novels dealing with women to corroborate the truthfulness of descriptions, motives and psychological states.[16]) Gironella is more at home in portraying a man's world, for most of his female characters are pawns in a thoroughly masculine environment. The author, however, describes women well only when he presents their physical characteristics: "Olga's hair was jet black, short and sleek. Her eyes were large and beautiful. She was slender, but with fully developed muscles and gave the impression of having a well proportioned body. . . ."[17]

As the novel progresses, Ignacio's character appears more clearly with a system of moral values very much like our author's. Thus, after the death of his billiard-playing friend Ernesto and sexual advances made by Doña Amparo, the Police Chief's wife, "Ignacio, in spite of the bank, Julio García, David, Olga, of everything, continued to cherish in his soul several relics: love for his family, chastity. He must go on living."[18] Ignacio is caught in a sexual and political whirlwind. Searching for a confidant, he seeks advice from David and Olga Pol. Communists, they point out their dissatisfactions with the Republic. In a harrowing scene the three visit an overcrowded and antiquated mental asylum. Gironella discusses the need for institutional reform because of ever-increasing problems of mental illness in Spain. Descriptions of the decay and destruction of other "institutions" such as the wrecking of Gerona's leading newspapers contributes to the Anarchist-Monarchist controversy and active war.

The Alvear family retreats to the church realizing that Gerona's socio-economic structure is tottering. The Alvears, like Gironella, reflect multiple attitudes about Catholicism that appear indecisive. Matías Alvear is agnostic. He recognizes that his wife's beliefs are based on tradition but does not know himself in what to believe. In a conversation between Mosén Alberto and Ignacio on faith, Ignacio confronts the priest openly with "intellectualizations" of faith, to the chagrin of the entire family. Tension fills the room but the conversation is disregarded by the family, especially by Matías, who would rather play dominos. His reactions to Ignacio's statements are quiet, stoical, typically Spanish. Without religious conviction, Matías has an excellent sense of balance because of his age and experience and delights in feverish discussions, no matter how devastating the consequences. He is much like Zorba, the Greek. His wife, however, cannot forgive Ignacio for his religious opinions or sexual indiscretions and remonstrates with him. Disputes such as these cause Ignacio's alienation from his family.

Gironella is equally at home in portrayal of the upper classes of Gerona who determine its social, economic and political structure. In physical descriptions of leading aristocrats such as Don Santiago de Estrada, Gironella also elaborates on their attitudes concerning their position, descrediting by implication rather than by direct attack. "[Don Santiago de Estrada] . . . considered his estates like a gift (for which he thanked his lucky stars), a means which permitted him to dedicate himself to politics and to tennis, both of which constituted his grand passions."[19] He is aware that aristocratic power exerts enormous influence over the Spanish masses. The first active protest, however, against the aristocracy occurs when the newspaper, *El Tradicionalista,* is destroyed by the Communists. Gironella describes the growth of political parties in Gerona with special attention given to the Communists. Cosme Vila and his henchman *El Responsable* are stereotypes who are political pawns for Russia.

Unlike the historical novels of Galdós and Balzac, those of Gironella de-emphasize individual qualities of his minor personages and subordinate their roles to a larger context—the revelation of the Alvears' personal drama. Thus, when the Falange becomes powerful in Madrid, its platform is echoed by José Alvear but does not affect his Catalan relatives who are deeply involved in their own provincial problems. Ignacio finally completes his lawyer's *Bachillerato*. César dedicates himself to the priesthood and Pilar enjoys her youth, going to movies with her girlfriends while all about the political situation worsens. The Falangists emerge politically the strongest nationally. The Republican Government is passive as Spanish Fascism gains.

We are always aware of the passage of time in the novel because of the convention of fixed dates that comprises its structure and because of the change of seasons. With the school recess, the entire Alvear family moves to its summer resort, San Feliü de Guíxols. Ignacio's experiences there are highly erotic and adolescent. "The first sensation he had upon going outside and finding himself alone was living one absolute moment in its entire fullness. The ocean at night created an inexplicable pleasure on his skin, a jubilant rhythm in his blood, a strange intellectual illumination that made him receptive to any message from the sea."[20] On the beach, Ignacio enjoys his first flirtation with Ana María and a series of summer entertainments—the circus, the puppet shows, the cinema. Their meeting and eventual separation is written with great delicacy and restraint.

Through letters to Ignacio from his parents, Gironella expresses parental concern but, after a few short-lived experiences, Ignacio returns to his studies and questions the meaning of faith. Gironella again justifies his religious skepticism. Ignacio temporarily accepts David Pol's Voltaireian solution, *il faut cultiver notre jardin*, suggesting there is no method by which to resolve the problem of faith. The narrative shifts to Collell where César contemplates God and studies in solitude. Between these polarities Gironella is to be found, embracing both arguments and unable to make a final decision.

Ignacio fears for César's safety because signs of revolution are

evident everywhere. Strikes break out because of hunger with
an undercurrent of fear. During these eventful days, Ignacio
corresponds with Ana María. David and Olga discourage him
because of Ana María's aristocratic background but Ignacio continues to seek her out. After a first kiss, Ignacio feels he has
reached maturity: "One day, Ignacio couldn't stand it anymore
and kissed her. He kissed her with outrageous force. She was
totally bewildered and could hardly remember the preceding
eighteen minutes of his sermon on chastity."[21]

Home from Barcelona, Ignacio receives a surprise gift of law
texts for his elementary courses. In a moving scene, Ignacio
realizes his responsibility to himself. He returns to work at the
Arús Bank and studies law, dismissing thoughts of Ana María
with his family's warm approval. Ana María persists in writing
but in vain since Ignacio has become increasingly interested in
local politics and does not reply to her letters. With politics
uppermost in every Spaniard's mind, Gironella seizes another
opportunity for description of prewar ideologies. Although one
critic thought that ". . . the real story of *The Cypresses Believe in
God* is the history of Spain"[22] and another considered it ". . . a
novel that offers sufficient facts, true information to study the
economic situation, the social level and the characteristics of
groups which existed at the time of the Republic on the 14th of
April, 1931 . . . ,"[23] it is still basically a *novel* that vividly drama-
tizes the coming of the war through the eyes of the Alvears.

The Alvears witness demonstrations by Masons flying "¡Viva
Cataluña Libre!" pennants; the Republican Army marches into
Gerona and a state of war is declared; secession from the Republic is put down after a bloody armed rebellion; political prisoners
are detained. All political prisoners are deprived of tobacco and
food. Despite Ignacio's joy that the rebellion did not succeed,
the fact of political prisoners under duress in the worst possible
health conditions aggravates and stirs up further discontent.
David and Olga Pol are jailed and await trial with hundreds of
other prisoners. The Alvears help them, providing them with
food throughout their time in prison. The Tribunal, the revolt
of Asturian miners, Franco's rebellion in North Africa, the burning of the Asturian Library of 300,000 volumes—all are summed
up in the words of Matías Alvear: "Of what things is man
capable of."[24] While active rebellion threatens, the Festival of

Narcissus, precautionary arrests, and preparations for the Tribunal are the background for Ignacio's study of law, and Ignacio's schoolmate, Mateo Santos, becomes one of the novel's leading personages because of his love for Pilar Alvear. A gay, young school girl whose chief preoccupations are her studies, her selection of a coiffure, a garment, or a boy, Gironella indicates that she is of a stronger and finer mettle to be tested in the future.

The Cypresses stretches fictional material over many chapters before reaching a conclusion. Gironella constantly shifts the narrative towards a new problem or personage and so assures continuity. Serious events like Gironella's depiction of the activities of the Tribunal are tightly written and dramatically portray the landed gentry's reactions to the masses and to the Separatist Movement. With the Tribunal as a political forum for revolutionary perspectives, Gironella attempts impartiality, presenting several points of view, permitting the reader to judge the merits of each platform for himself. Despite Gironella's claim of impartiality, he favors the Falange, choosing Mateo Santos (son of the aristocrat Don Emilio Santos) to present the ideals of the Falange in a speech to his father:

The Falange was a revolutionary organization! Much more revolutionary than any of the Syndicates, which limited themselves to promising better economic conditions. The Falange claimed first, to convince the producers that they were not the proletariat but men, persons. Second, they tried to explain to them that economic factors are not everything, that apart from satisfying the bare necessities, there are a thousand spiritual roads by which to progress. Third, they tried to make men love their families and their work. Fourth, they gave them a similar "collective illusion" of life. Fifth, they made them understand the meaning of their native land.[25]

This summary is Gironella's most vivid presentation of any platform in the entire novel and such a youthful idealization of the Falange as Mateo's was apparently the basis for the appeal of Spain's new political and economic frontier of the 1930's. Ignacio realizes that Falange is synonymous with Fascism and cannot understand Mateo's dedication to such convictions.

When a local citizen, Joaquín Santaló, admits killing Pedro Oriol, also son of an aristocrat, his conviction and execution by the Tribunal result in a violent Communist response. The Falange emerges from obscurity when Communists, reacting to the injustice of Joaquín Santaló's execution, decide to set fire to the forests around Gerona. Their burning of Gerona's forests is a truly symbolic act because the very cypresses for César are conducive to belief in God. Gironella suggests here that a godless Spain is in the offing. Violence begets violence and Communist incendiary reaction and Falange counterreaction destroy the soul. Ignacio's political attitudes remain unclear since he believes each Spaniard will develop an individual interpretation of the war, surviving because of his own moral strength. "It is man who succumbs, not history. History is only tribulation in which people are shaped by their actions or are deprived of their authority. The Spaniard, without ideas has succumbed; he has been deprived."[26] For Gironella believes the individual will triumph over the collective.

Christmas festivals, Ignacio's birthday celebration, a snowfall in Gerona, provide brief interludes to violence and political strife. For a novel of such Gargantuan proportions, Gironella repeats or restates very little, with one outstanding exception—his emphasis upon the Falange platform. He summarizes the political situation at the end of 1933: "Spain finds itself divided first into geographical regional separatism, second, because of the struggle between political parties and third, because of class struggles. Always the number three. The world is full of trinities. Trinities of fortune: faith, hope and charity; Gaspar, Melchior, Balthasar. . . . Trinities of evil: Freemasons, Judaism, Communism. . . ."[27] In this connection, Chapter XXXIX emphasizes rewards for participation in the Falange and probably was inserted into the novel to insure publication.

Descriptions of historical events and political intrigues alternate with fiction when the writer returns to the Alvears: Ignacio's preposterous affair with Canela, his gonorrhea, his confession to please Carmen Elgazu. His confessor advises Ignacio to order his life. This is a common problem to all Gironellan heroes and thus, insistence on happiness, optimism, faith in nature, God, and himself are values that make Gironella an "inspirational" novelist and *The Cypresses* inspiring. "For Gironella, permanence resides in the conscious responsibility of every man. This personal vision of life, of the world, of history is the reason and greatness of Gironella's literary work. . . . He is the only novelist that has concerned himself with our future."[28] On occasion, the author seems overenthusiastic when he discusses Catalan patriotism or when he writes of elemental truths in his natural and unsophisticated prose. A reader may well be tempted to say, "How typical, how beautiful and how simple life really is!" *The Cypresses* and its epic proportions do not eclipse the integrity of its simple people. It is a novel about families. Gironella believes the integral social unit of Spain is the family. So readers are always informed of the activities of all the Alvears. Separately their individual stories weave in the aggregate the entire fabric of the narrative. Thus, César's experiences are never neglected despite physical removal from his family. Occasional chapters describe his spiritual growth in the seminary and it is always evident César possesses too beautiful a soul for earth. Gironella forewarns us of César's ultimate tragedy (or glory) by association of him with "... the revolution and blood, the cypresses and bones."[29]

Gironella also adds details to descriptions of many of Gerona's leading citizens, among them, the Police Chief, Julio García, a major commentator of the political arguments of the Café el Neutral. He predicts the downfall of the Communists although he believes in their goals and studies the social scene, feeding on the weaknesses of others as did Vautrin of Balzac's novels. It is inevitable that this Machiavelli will survive the war.

Midpoint in the novel, Gironella narrows the ideological conflicts to the Communists under Cosme Vila against the Falange and Mateo Santos. He expends greater attention upon Mateo's faction. When Ignacio attends one of the Falange meetings in anticipation of becoming a member, each member of the Falange is described in detail. He remains aloof although his companions are politically active. Mateo and Ignacio pass their law examinations at the University of Barcelona and continue their friendship. The Alvears rejoice with Ignacio in his success and César, home from Collell on vacation, hardly eats or sleeps because of his constant search for God.

The life-death struggle is of primary thematic concern in *The Cypresses*. It is presented symbolically—burning of forests, poisoning of rivers, droughts, and realistically—the death of the spirit. Death as a negative stimulus forces Gironella's protagonists to react more vitally to life. Most deaths in the novel are referred to in retrospect—the suicide of an old man plunging

from a balcony to a stone street of the Ramblas or the death of
José Luis de Soria in combat. Although such effects appear
incidental to the plot, they motivate the action. Thus, José Luis's
tragedy causes his sister Marta to participate actively in the
Falange with Mateo Santos.

Gironella's interest in reporting significant international events
while the Civil War continues is of importance because it stresses
how the Spanish intellectual is cognizant of other nations' politics
and problems. In 1935, When Mussolini invaded Abyssinia, its
political ramifications become the theme of Spanish political
discussions. So too, Naziism, Fascism, National-Socialism and
their ideologies and effects figure in the context of European
politics. One critic opposes Gironella's inclusion of such documentation: "Without amplification of his perspectives, Gironella's
view of what is happening is reduced to journalism, more or less
faithful to the events but never profound. Because of this excessive preoccupation with documentation, newspaper reporting
and eyewitness accounts, Gironella's novel suffers. His characters
lack authenticity because they are only functional creations. . . .
In the final analysis, it's always bad to sacrifice the artistic elements of a novel to journalism."[30]

Against a background of national revolts, strikes, army insur-
rections, the scheduled elections proceed while the Alvears
tensely await their outcome. Ignacio's ideological conflict between traditional and liberal views appears clear: "Two Spains
are face to face—the one of Unamuno, Carmen Elgazu, the Com-
mandant Martínez de Soria and the other of Julio García, David
and Olga, Giner de los Ríos, Ramón y Cajál and *El Responsable,*
the one of Ignacio listening to Mosén Alberto.[31] Gironella contrasts proponents for political traditionalism, peace, and the economic status quo with those favoring liberalism, socialist reform,
and modernization.

Gironella not only stresses the complexity of Spanish politics
and the inevitability of Civil War, he also explains the rebellion
in less than adequately documented conclusions. "There is more
fanaticism here than anywhere else. Pure ideas are personified
immediately into flesh and blood. . . . The structure of democracy
sways everywhere because of natural wear and tear of the system
and because it fell under control of the Jews. . . ."[32] The strong
convictions of his characters, nevertheless, give strength to their

opinions and establish the author's persuasive power as a novelist rather than as an historian. For example, if Ignacio Alvear is
unclear about his political commitment, he is strongly convinced
of his love for Marta de Soria, a Falangist leader. Gironella ties
in their romance with the successes of the Falange. In later chapters the Falange appears strong after the destruction of churches
by the Communists, the breakdown of aristocratic power, and
the termination of unjust national policies such as those repress-
ing Catalonia for many years. When José Antonio, leader of the
Falange, is slain in Madrid, the repercussions of his death are felt
throughout Spain.

Gironella recreates the tension in the lives of Gerona's citizens.
Mateo's imprisonment and José Antonio's assassination precipi-
tate the outbreak of hostilities. With electric, gas and water sup-
plies cut off, the anarchy which formerly prevailed becomes
revolution. The political factions responsible for the revolution
are no longer of importance. Bombs are exploded and men die.
The entire Alvear family is trapped in the full tide of revolution.
Pilar sees Mosén Alberto's Diocesan Museum blown up and a
dead body for the first time. Matías reconciles the horror of daily
calamaties realistically: "... Life goes on."[33]

Gironella's great attention to visual effects is impressive. War
transforms the now familiar Gerona of his imagination—its architectural plan, its monuments, churches, streets, cemeteries. The
burial, traditionally Spanish, of the first war victims is especially
moving. Each tombstone is a reminder of the casualties of past
wars and the stately elegance and serenity of the cypresses cannot console those who mourn.

Ignacio attends a few Communist meetings to judge their platform. Apparently, Gironella is decidedly sympathetic to the aims
of the Falange for Communists appear as a stereotyped group of
petty gangsters dependent upon Russian infiltration, espionage,
and support. To demonstrate resistance to the Falange, Commu-
nist-inspired strikes and bombing raids destroy lives and property with the Catholic Church as scapegoat. Church bombings,
even death in church desecrations, strike home to the Alvears
because of César, their seminarian son.

Meanwhile, Ignacio takes his final law examinations at the
University of Barcelona. The Republican Government continues
its middle-of-the-road policy as a desire for Franco to establish

order in chaos appeals to Communists and Falange alike. Gironella develops three themes simultaneously: the personal lives of
the Alvears, the local political situation in Gerona, and national
events of Spain. Julián Marías notes this same point but expresses
his view differently:

In Gironella, we find a vivid, careful intent to depict all planes of
perspective. [*The Cypresses Believe in God* is . . .] a chronicle and refers precisely to the transformation of Spanish life during the years of
the Spanish Republic. . . . This novel is saturated with important personal references to the immediate present, to minor matters and the
most trivial ones as well and how they manifest themselves within the
political and social realities of the day and not symbolically as it had
been feared. . . . I have said at times that the novel contains pure narration with all the details. We must add that Gironella's novel is superior in form to all the others of its kind because it does not neglect any
essential dimension of the circumstances, because everything functions
dynamically within the narrative.[34]

Gironella's rigid adherence to a preconceived stylistic pattern
allows for very little prose variation. Apparently Gironella has
schematized his personages purposely, making them symbolic of
all individuals and their struggles in Spain. An alternation of
three points of view for a total panorama of Spanish life is difficult since some incidents may not serve Gironella's original fictional purpose. In *The Cypresses* much historical documentation
could be excised easily, thus reducing the size of the work and
giving it cohesion. Although the novel provides enough accurate
historical and economic information for an historical document,[35]
The Cypresses is too broad. Gironella might have concentrated
on fewer events and characters. As it is, a growing list of characters with those of the sequels, *One Million Dead* and *The Peace
Has Broken Out* makes it probable that Gironella prefers breadth
to depth in the recreation of a social climate.

After passing the first half of his law examinations, Ignacio
will not complete his studies. Unable to be insensitive to events,
he is forced to take a stand on political issues. His friend, Mateo,
fearing for his life, escapes into hiding. Franco is rumored to
have taken command of the Canary Islands. The Civil Guard
remains powerful in Barcelona. Communists and Falange leaders plan to assassinate Martínez de Soria and to burn the mon-
astery at Collell. The murder of Calvo Sotelo ends the power of

the Republican Government. Civil war finally breaks out: "Ignacio saw the writing on the wall."[36] "Julio understood the die was cast."[37] With these pronouncements, *The Cypresses Believe in God* moves to its swift conclusion.

All political factions marshall their forces for the inevitable conflict. Ignacio, as usual, intellectualizes: "Ignacio had come to one conclusion after all these events: the prevailing atmosphere angered his brain."[38] Franco assumes authority and appears in heroic terms: "For the glory of God, for the force and power that reside in Him! To the glorious hero, blessed in combat, soul and heart! To General Franco!"[39] Barcelona falls to Falangist control as Communists burn churches and kill priests. Gironella describes the unleashing of hostilities in Gerona and whereabouts and actions of all major and minor characters. In one of his final chapters, Gironella reports some thirty-six deaths. "Everything occurred with overwhelming simplicity in the silence of the night: the squeak of the tires, the feeling of cold, violent shoves towards an unknown wall on which there were countless niches, the vague trembling of some cypresses, footsteps, the sound of bolts of guns, a mutual embrace, shots and then death."[40]

César is separated from his family. The Revolutionary Committee detains him because of his attempts to preserve consecrated hosts by swallowing them. The Alvears hear of his arrest and Ignacio tries to save him. As a dangerous threat to the new order, César is executed with a large group of political prisoners, thus achieving the martyrdom he had desired. His death, however, serves no purpose other than to accentuate the confusion of the political situation. "And then César heard a shot and he felt something sweet penetrate his skin."[41] César dies an "El Greco-like figure," incarnating "the reality of charity which is where God is."[42] Shot down with one hundred other prisoners, the writer does not moralize upon his death although it is a triple tragedy: the family of Alvear has lost a son, Spain has lost a useful citizen, and the Civil War has wasted another life.

II *Appraisal of Gironella's First Civil War Novel*

Despite its melodrama, extensive descriptions of political ideologies, stereotyped minor characters and unimportant family episodes, *The Cypresses Believe in God* is one of the best novels

to come out of Spain in the past fifteen years. Gironella has
attempted to impose not only a cosmos on the chaos of the Civil
War years but adds an epic tone for historic events in the tradition of the great generation novels of Balzac and Galdós. An
excellent observer, he can photographically recreate an entire
world, typically Spanish and authentic in his description of
Spain's bourgeoisie. One critic has praised his portrayal of the
Alvears: "The Alvear family will remain in the history of our
literature as the best example, the most complete, the most perfect, the best studied portrait of our middle class."[43]

The Cypresses also displays Gironella's sense for unified composition and an integrated whole. His earlier novels demonstrate
his ability to describe but with little discipline to select detail
or theme. In *The Cypresses* he limits himself sensibly (despite
the 871-page length of the novel), avoiding sententious and
repetitious passages. The fusion of his characters is another improvement. Elements of fact and fiction are so well blended in
The Cypresses that most critics cannot distinguish between
biography and imagination. Gironella's care in tracing lives and
deeds and their movements through the whirlwind of historical
and political events create the grandiose, epic quality of the
novel.

Character is also continually shaped through experience. Each
minor personage represents a problem of Spain in miniature. In
fact, "every episode, every fact, every character, real or fictional,
serves one purpose in the novel, to present the story of Spain's
struggle with herself."[44] Nevertheless, they are never vital because they are representative of political ideologies, grey figures,
"caricatures, thinly-drawn protagonists, nihilistic war mongers
. . . despite the gypsy color, the quick violence, the fulminating
strength of all its extremists. . . ."[45] Still, his major personages,
the Alvears, are his truly important creations because of their
intrinsic Spanish qualities. Nevertheless, some critics, like Mark
Van Doren, believe that Ignacio is a transparent creature, "without convictions of his own. He is a lens through which the reader
looks at the innumerable parties of opinion, among whose articu-
late members he strolls. . . ."[46] Or, as to Gironella, some feel "he
has not made a careful study, nor has he delved deeply into the
psychological reasons or reactions of his characters."[47] The
Alvears do not represent real people but exist as façades who

wear social labels, types.[48] Such remarks do not account for the success of Gironella's portrayal of Ignacio because the hero is a character composite of the influences which have shaped him. His central role is to report the prejudices, intellectual convictions, and psychologies of those he encounters, creating an organic view of Spain through his own relationship to the war. There is nothing static about his personality.

Ignacio is a symbol of two Spains—one struggling for wider European influence, the other retaining its irrational, fanatical traditions. Ignacio is not a conceptual hero but an anti-hero, living on the margin of political and social events,[49] and his chief problem is the dualism of choice between reason and emotion. Even so, Ignacio's lack of emotion or Gironella's refusal to provide him with strong, passionate feelings is the chief failing of the novel. "The defects we would like to point out about José María Gironella's work: failure to give believable emotions to his characters, to have been impartial, to have been unjust . . . ; but who knows if these defects, in the last analysis, were not among the great virtues of *The Cypresses Believe in God*. Gironella's view of life is excellently portrayed in the novel."[50] The novel is truthful and realistic when his personages do not surrender readily to purely fictional events. And if Gironella's prose be uneven, erratic, or lacking at times in sustained quality, it presents the realities of his Spain. Gironella's personages act and talk like real Spaniards—naturally, sympathetically, realistically. His style is terse and direct, stripped of all aesthetic pretensions and, therefore, effective. It creates a "sense of participation which the author's skill gives to the reader."[51]

The Cypresses Believe in God is not a defense or condemnation of the war but an ambitious realistic novel. Gironella does no direct moralizing nor does he draw conclusions. He is an observer seeking answers to his own questions about the war and leaving to his readers their own thoughts and conclusions.

In the face of clerical opposition, certain critics consider *The Cypresses* a Catholic novel about "a country in which the beautiful and holy are never completely lost, that is, a nation emotional both in its family and its national affairs."[52] For them the message of the novel is "that to be Catholic in the properly understood sense of the word is to make sense out of the world and to have peace."[53] Others feel the genesis of *The Cypresses* results

from the author's own political negativism: "Gironella's novel
stems from pessimism, an anti-romantic view and a certain un-
formulated constructive intent. His pessimism is not an attitude
nor a philosophy that derives from the reality of politics. Rather,
it is born in his distrust of political parties and their programs."[54]
Still others feel that Gironella wrote a blend of truth and fiction
which appraises the problems of the war fairly accurately. It is
far more judicious to believe that *The Cypresses* originated as
a natural outgrowth of the writer's personal necessity to come to
terms with himself and his generation. Gironella emphasizes one
truth—in spite of the great tragedy of Civil War, man can retain
his dignity and, whatever his own particular social or political
commitment, perceive the honor and virtue that existed on both
sides. This novel and its sequel are based on the author's personal ethic of sincerity. *The Cypresses Believe in God* is not a
mere phenomenon continuing the Galdósian tradition of the
realist novel.

CHAPTER 5

Death and Un millón de muertos
(One Million Dead)

I *Prominence of theDeath Theme in*
One Million Dead

JOSÉ María Gironella's sequel, *Un millón de muertos* (*One Million Dead*), continues and amplifies the vicissitudes of the Alvear family of *The Cypresses Believe in God,* alternating like its predecessor fiction with condensed resumés of historical data. It suffers equally from Gironella's attempt to include all phases of the war. It is excellent in almost photographic narrative and in dramatic dialogue.

An introductory note deprecates the value of a sequel, holding that to appreciate it, *The Cypresses* is an essential predecessor. On the contrary, *One Million Dead* is separate and distinct from *The Cypresses.* It is a chronicle of the war years and a panorama of Spain fought over by Nationalists and Communists. *One Million Dead* is designed to correct the errors of foreign authors such as André Malraux, Arthur Koestler and Ernest Hemingway, and their explanations of the Spanish Civil War. Gironella's essential theme is life and death. Appropriately 500,000 actually died in the war but Gironella prefers to name his sequel *One Million Dead* to include another half-million of the spiritually dead as well. Thus, *One Million Dead* is more than a mere continuation of *The Cypresses.* The embryo of his considerations on life and death is realized to the fullest in his sequel.

In *The Cypresses,* Gironella describes his countrymen dying in rioting, strikes, church burnings. Death is anonymous and objective. "The last two catastrophies that fell on the city affected a smaller number of people but were, nevertheless, irreparable. They had but one common outcome—death!"[1] "At dawn, all thirty-six were murdered in ditches or by the trees on the road and

were left there without burial."² "At his side stood an entire
family, including a woman fingering her rosary beads. Cosme
Vila came close to the wall and began firing his machine gun.
Ta-ta-ta-ta-ta. The family fell one by one."³ "The bodies of Don
Santiago Estrada and his wife, those of the Assistant Director of
the bank and his brother Juan, the bodies of Don Jorge, his wife,
all their children and servants; everyone was there except Jorge,
who was in the Pyrenees...."⁴

Death historically true to fact, such as that of Calvo Sotelo, is
treated dispassionately: "The Director of the cemetery in Madrid
communicated with the Town Hall that at five in the morning a
body was left there for burial. It was Calvo Sotelo."⁵ Nevertheless, a death witnessed by the Alvears always seems to have a
true meaning for the author, and for his readers. Just as, in *The
Cypresses*, Joaquín Santaló is brutally shot down by a firing
squad, so César Alvear is murdered. Both deaths are as realistic
as poetic and César's death even takes on the dimensions of
martyrdom. There are also striking stylistic harmonies to be
found in the prose descriptive of the deaths of Joaquín Santaló
and César: "The cemetery was the place selected. The river next
to it lapped up the essences of the dead. When the echo of shots
faded after they rebounded off the tombs, they approached
Montjuich and arrived at the Hermitage of the Angels; there in
the plot of the Costa family and of Laura, in the chants that
presided over the city, they heard a rhythm of hammers. The
masons began their song of the mountains...."⁶ "Then César
heard a shot and felt something sweet penetrate his skin....
Later his eyes closed. He felt a kiss on his brow. Then his heart
stopped forever."⁷

Readers are forewarned of César's death and his martyrdom:
"It is true César entered into the precincts of the dead, treading
lightly. His father may have made a mistake, believing he was
morbid. His attitude towards death was familiar. He felt simply
that he was surrounded by brothers. He viewed the crosses on
the ground without thinking they were grievous blows."⁸ "The
boy, since he had arrived at Collell, had an obsession. What was
there in that boy whose language was superior to that of the
canons? He was obsessed because he had discovered something
more important than his work in Braca Street; he had discovered
that César wanted to die.... César wanted to achieve the su-

preme act, that of giving his life."[9] Envisaging death poetically,
Gironella heightens his symbolism by personifying its brooding
spirit. "By midmorning, the phantom of death hovered over the
city. A collective feeling of responsibility haunted the people."[10]
So too he unites it to his physical and spiritual landscapes. The
cemetery and its surrounding cypresses are for him the realities
to symbolize death in both novels. Antithetically, these also
express the essences of life.

With regard to the mountains, César didn't understand it. "How
could anybody set fire to the mountains?" he thought. In Collell, César
rhapsodized over the mountains and would never forget them during
Christmas when they were covered with snow. About the trees, at
times he believed they had souls! . . . he saw the leaves of the black
poplars stirring in the breeze, greeting him or at other times they
seemed to cry. "No one was capable of burning them deliberately,"
he thought. And of course, he had not thought about the cypresses,
which according to his understanding, were the trees that had more
reasons to believe in God.[11]

He rarely sentimentalizes but perceives the realities of physical
degeneration as a consequence of death: ". . . a total of thirty-six
bodies were converted into food for worms. . . ."[12] Death is to be
met simply, silently, even unexpectedly. Like his Jorge Manrique,
Gironella alludes to death's levelling function: "Everyone stopped
breathing, especially our own Mateo. It had never occurred to
them to make such a distinction; they were all so accustomed to
believe that death made all human beings totally equal."[13] As he
describes the murdered body of Joaquín Santaló, Gironella emphasizes the brutality of the deed and recounts its details. He
points out the dichotomy between physical and spiritual, between body and soul. "He was afraid of seeing Joaquín with his
throat cut, his tongue torn out of his mouth, his heart thrown on
to the sands of the sea in a place where the ocean would cover
and uncover it twice a day and his body reduced to ashes and
these ashes scattered over the surface of the ground."[14]

His body appeared to be enormously reduced in size. He remembered
his friend's voice, his peculiar manner of swearing. Now he was in
front of Joaquín's body, stiff, with his nose pointing towards the
heavens. He looked so dry, so dead, like a mineral that Ignacio thought
Joaquín's heart had simply stopped beating when he died. But Ignacio
was wrong. Something deeper had occurred to Joaquín at the moment

of death. Something fled from him, something that you couldn't touch. It wasn't physical but more vital than blood, air or the brain. Clearly, his sould surrendered to the Lord. His saintly spirit fled from his body to be resurrected.[15]

Gironella sees Ernesto Oriol's body as dry, material residue after death overcame a once vital organism. Death is an end to the physical being but the soul is a unified, separate and spiritual entity, existing apart from the body. Since Gironella does not indicate Ernesto's soul has returned to God, he prefers to describe the physical nature of life.

Death is a natural and sometimes accidental occurrence. "But the old man kept on moving forward through the dining room and repeated: 'Why? I didn't do anything here. Perhaps it's better to go to America.' And he continued moving forward until he crossed the threshold of the open balcony. He stumbled against the railing and suddenly it gave way because of his weight. He disappeared, smashing against the stones of Barca Street."[16] Gironella describes an old man's tragic and possibly suicidal fall. Fascinated by suicides, he enjoys describing suicidal tendencies. In fact, his Chief of Police, Julio García, is a specialist in "suicides." His David and Olga Pol, children of parents who committed suicide, tell Ignacio about "a strange man who built a marvelous model of Barcelona's Columbus Monument in miniature out of cork. He lived alone and one night, a Japanese ship entered the harbor. He went to the lighthouse and he hanged himself."[17] This tale is purely incidental and so is suicide rare among Spaniards. Gironella's preoccupation, like Julio García's, seems caused by his intellectualization of suicide.

Gironella is not only attracted by death from natural causes, from exterior circumstances, from mental perturbation, but also by infliction of death in wartime. "The majority of militiamen were surprised to find that to kill one man or five was equally easy. Just think of the word 'fascist,' aim at the heart or head and fire, nothing more."[18] He describes the varying attitudes of prisoners about to die as well. "The imminence of death brought to the condemned a feeling of relief and a sense of importance. Some, however, crept along like lizards, filled with loathing. Others showed an unfathomable calm and a strange precision in each movement as if each gesture had been thought about over the years. This self-control was evident even as they bowed their heads before the firing squad."[19] If the death motif occupies a prime position in *The Cypresses* and *One Million Dead*, it is because as a young man, the sight of death affected him during the Civil War years.[20] Gironella-Ignacio Alvear (as he says he is) must have witnessed many tragedies, losing at least a "spiritual" brother in the war. Sight of so many deaths convinces Gironella of the value of life. He stresses death because he feels the living must be continually reminded of their errors, their fallibility, their past deeds. The dead, consequently, remind and commemorate the errors of war. Death thus serves life, and the theme of Cain and Abel, symbols of man's struggle with his neighbor, his brother and himself, is a leitmotif of *One Million Dead*.

Gironella's introduction to *One Million Dead* reveals his conscientiousness. He composed three separate versions before establishing the definitive text. The aim of the first version is to "... put the events into chronological order and ... edit a kind of catalogue of horrors."[21] His second version eliminates the banal and lyrically intensifies action. The final version achieves both aims and adds a feeling for truth. *One Million Dead* accomplishes these three purposes admirably. With a tremendous amount of historical research, interviews with observers, culling of photographic and film materials, *One Million Dead* purports to be a novel, not an historical essay. Nevertheless, during the six-year period Gironella worked on this novel, his original ideas changed as fictional intrigues gave way to concentration on historical data and caused controversy as to whether Gironella is novelist, historian, or a combination of both. One critic has made this perspicacious commentary: "[The novel] decreases even more the actions of independent characters who possessed vitality in *The Cypresses Believe in God*. Therefore, this book loses much as a novel. [It is] an orderly chronicle of the Civil War."[22]

II   *Analysis of Structure, Plot and Characters of* One Million Dead

One Million Dead in four parts covers the period July 30, 1936 to April 1, 1939. Gironella wisely included a resumé of leading characters noting their roles in the novel. He begins his sequel in the cemetery where César is about to be buried. Gironella describes Ignacio's discovery of his brother's body in the setting, the light, the events taking place in and around Gerona at the height of civil war. In his fascination with the death theme, he reports gruesome details of César's tragedy and Ignacio's reactions thereto: "César lay on the ground with his legs separated, his shoulders turned inward and was terrifyingly immobile."[23] "César's head was thrown back and Ignacio saw that one of his ears was incredibly yellow in color. César's body was cold. His face was in perfect repose.... He was disfigured, a coagulated mass."[24] Ignacio's first impulse is to flee. Taking César's religious medal from around his neck, he embraces the corpse and leaves without thinking of prayer. Chapter I concludes melodramatically Ignacio's problem in the closing pages of *The Cypresses*—could Ignacio arrive in time to save César from the firing squad? This chapter describes as well Ignacio's feelings on death when it finally touches the Alvears. César's death and death itself is the underlying theme for the entire novel.

Chapter after chapter, Gironella interpolates the military strategy of the Falange, the Communists, and the International Brigades in a welter of superfluous, historical data and secondary experiences. An occasional passage reflects the family's attitude towards war. The Alvears are neutral, feeling only their grief. "At times, Matías, while walking through the streets, felt a kind of shudder when he saw a group of militiamen. He looked at them one by one, trying to discover which one shot down his son César."[25] Each of the family must reconcile César's death to his or her own life. "Blessed Pilar! She was a pure thing, too young for that world of ghosts. She was the only one whose eyes seemed to be able to look at the world innocently."[26] César's death prompts Ignacio to assert himself as a bitter critic of war, its futility, and the power of the collective. Seeking a philosophy so typical of all Gironellan heroes, Ignacio becomes politically engagé as political parties consolidate in Gerona. His sweetheart, Marta de Soria, a Falange Activist Leader, forced into hiding in Barcelona, declares her intention to Ignacio of escaping into France. Gironella's treatment of the escape scene is full-blown melodrama: "Will you wear braids?" "Sure," she answered. "That's a stupendous idea." "You should put on dark glasses as well. And don't carry any packages. Just wear a blouse and skirt of gaudy, bright colors," he replied."[27] Her farewell scene with Ignacio is also in the best "cloak and dagger" tradition. Marta is able to make good her escape through Julio García's efforts. Julio's views show in a conversation with a Communist-in-hiding, Doctor Relkin, while visiting Barcelona to help Marta make her escape from Spain. When he declares the Germans to be a cruel, heartless race who can exterminate an entire population callously, Gironella draws a parallel to the Spanish problem but presents another view of death, showing how the Civil War is distinct: "In Spain, there is a deep-seated necessity for killing more so here than in any other place because people believe that death is not the end of things but a simple journey or another imagined eternal life."[28]

Besides discussion of life-death dualism, *One Million Dead* develops the problem of spiritual and physical solitude. César's death leaves Ignacio immobile, alone, crushed by the overwhelming weight of loneliness. His chief problems are to explain his brother's untimely death, the Civil War, and to understand his own feelings of *soledad* (solitude). Ignacio cannot find any moral support in Catholicism, affirming Angel Ganivet's assertion that religion in Spain is out of contact with the spirit of the Spanish people: "The religion we preach in Spain has been terribly sad and defensive.... What occurs is that the commandments of God's law do not work. They are against our instincts, and in a country like ours, sensual by nature, they prove unbearable."[29] This Gironella offers as one explanation of the Civil War. Insights such as these are rarely found in the novel.

Alternating detailed chapters of fierce battle scenes with the Alvears' personal story, Gironella occasionally inserts philosophical commentaries, easily overlooked because of his ever-persistent documentation. "No one knew why they were fighting, everyone knew it. No one defended anything, everyone defended everything.... Nobody fought for abstract ideals. The only thing men could lay claim to was satisfaction of their juvenile appetites, or deep-seated egotisms."[30] Somewhat like a film director overlooking the melee of a war scene, Gironella remains above, coolly analytic, detached from the chaos below, trying to find the best possible presentation of the scene. As Miguel de Unamuno has the power to infuse life and death, so is Gironella a manipulator of lives and circumstances. Thus, he kills the anarchist Porvenir, making his fictional death serve to document the historically true

Communist acts of vengeance against the Civil Guard. Senseless reprisal follows senseless reprisal and these historical scenes are buttressed by appeals to national pride. Quoting the entire song, *La Internacional,* verbatim, he emphasizes patriotism and its emotional, affective values. He expresses through Ignacio his personal resentment against suppression of religion although he does not find consolation in prayer. "Much greatness and many shortcomings lay within us. We never changed and we are still no good. We conquered America, certainly; but what trifling results! Fatalism, the knife and the ready revolver. And why did we conquer America? For the same reasons that drove us into the war—for God, for the Devil and for the hell of it."[31] Civil war forced the Spaniard to assess what values are most important to him: "However, two things are certain: not to die in the war and to live and love."[32]

Gironella does make historical reportage palatable, for he evokes such feeling for truth and reality as almost to insure reliving the experience. Thus, one of Gironella's personages is present at the death of Federico García Lorca and his report of this tragedy lends greater significance and reality to the incident. Citation of García Lorca's verses emphasizes the tragedy of his execution. Colorful conversations by soldiers replete with the vulgarisms typical of wartime, such minor factual reports on the rise of venereal disease among the men, are indicative of conditions. These conversations also indicate humor and despair universal to soldiers in extended war novels. Soldiers' evaluation of reasons for fighting attest to Gironella's conclusion that the Spanish Civil War is an emotionally charged outlet for pent-up frustrations: "War was the answer for each person. It was their glory, defeat, prosperity and regeneration. And in many cases, their sweet sinking into eternity."[33] Remarks dispersed widely throughout the narrative reinforce his position: "He didn't impute the evils in Spain to laziness but to ignorance."[34] "War was more than calculation; it was also a kind of magic that would have vast repercussions in the future."[35] "War rejuvenates, although it may create the contrary as well. It excites our interest for something and makes us feel young. War has a meaning and therefore, while the forces are equal, there are no suicides. . . . Fighting now was not for scoring points but to save the country."[36] "Nobody knew up to what point what might be demanded of a man. At this moment it was fashionable to be a hero, to die early."[37]

Gironella's premise of impartiality in reporting events poses a problem. Before its first publication in Spain in 1961, the author said to Fernández Cuenca in an interview cited by J. J. Devlin: "The novel has been suspended for now and I fear it will continue to be so for several years. Because I believe that to be able to be absolutely impartial and just in narrating the events of our civil war, it is indispensable to avail oneself of the necessary perspective which I still lack."[38] *One Million Dead* demonstrates a detached perspective making the novel international in scope and, thus, atypical of the tradition of the Spanish novel. Gironella's analytical historical point of view and his cold neutrality are very evident. "José María Gironella tells us about the war in all of its phases although I believe that objectivity does not equal neutrality and that by taking on his shoulders all of the elements of judgment, he does not reveal his own opinion."[39]

His indirect approach has touched off controversies as to the historical aspects of *One Million Dead*. Joaquín Pérez Madrigal's *España a dos voces: los infundios y la historia* (*Spain's Two Voices: Fairy Tales and History*) attempts to correct Gironella's *fábulas urdidas* (contrived fables)[40] and, attacking him for falsifications, Madrigal condemns *One Million Dead* as the folly of a young novelist to which his work is a corrective. Moreover, Luis Emilio Sotelo, son of the late Calvo Sotelo, produced a series of articles impugning Gironella's work as to neutrality, historical accuracy and literary merit:

Gironella has written a book entitled *One Million Dead*, which epitomizes a climate of indifference, lukewarmness and dogmatic neutrality noted previously.... This manner of relating the story, saying the least and keeping silent on the most important events and even narrating the minor episodes without rigor or exactitude is a splendid demonstration of Gironella's "objectivity." ... Gironella's objectivity has a neutral meaning. ... *One Million Dead* is not an objective work. Certainly, its "epic values," the "brilliance" of its people is controlled capriciously throughout the novel.[41]

After examining *One Million Dead* from eight aspects which include its epic and tragic qualities, its personages, its chamber of horrors, Luis Emilio Calvo Sotelo offers Antonio Montero's

Historia de la persecución religiosa en España, 1936–39 (*History of Religious Persecution in Spain, 1936-39*) as the definitive and accurate historical document of the period, while *One Million Dead* should be read chiefly as a realist novel utilizing an historical base for creation of a cross section of humanity and ideology. For example, the historical objectivity of the deaths of Primo de Rivera and Benaventura Durruti appear less prominent because they are overshadowed by Marta de Soria's escape to freedom over the Pyrenees. Again, although the novel is largely political, the passage of time does not increase the Alvears' commitment to a particular political ideology. Gironella's constant emphasis is the strength of the individual family unit, the key to Spain's regeneration and in harmony with Nationalist policy.

Melodrama alternates with history as the lovers, Ignacio and Marta, are forced to separate. Thereafter, Marta meets Salvatore, an Italian soldier, and enters upon a fleeting relationship with him. This episode introduces an international element to the novel. German and Italian aid including the International Brigades are introduced through this personal involvement. It also affords an opportunity to evaluate Franco. "We consider him a good general, honest and capable of winning the war."[42] He and the Falange are always victorious and it has been noted that Gironella "... seems overly careful in sparing the feelings of the Falangists."[43]

Ignacio Alvear finally capitulates and enlists as a medical aide for the Nationalist Armies. Ignacio's experiences, as well as those of other members of the family are not forgotten, for Paz Alvear, Ignacio's cousin, becomes a spy for the Falange in Burgos and in Madrid, his cousin José is promoted to Chief Demolition Expert. Ignacio's journeys to Barcelona and Madrid, his role as saboteur, and his experiences with his wartime comrades conclude at the war's end in reunion with his family in Gerona.

Gironella creates many new characters. International reports as set forth by Fanny and Raymond Bolen, and a glimpse of Ernest Hemingway and Ilya Ehrenburg chatting in a bar on English poetry during a conflagration just outside Valencia are typical examples. The author presents "outsiders" and their point of view, who cannot really understand the Spanish Civil War: "Spain was puzzling, astonishing. I don't like Spain ... but it fascinates me."[44] One reporter sees Spain as a battleground for the axis powers and another as a land in civil strife because of ideological differences. Still, all acknowledge that "what's important is to know who will win."[45] Foreign reporters report atrocities photographically but the author continues to insist they cannot comprehend the war situation: "... The only thing reporters brought to Spain was a collection of devious tricks ... and two pairs of castanets."[46] Only Spaniards can understand Spain.[47]

When Guernica is bombed and party leaders flee the debris of a city reduced to rubble, Ignacio escapes from Barcelona to Madrid. There he meets his cousin José and realizes after long conversations that he does not share José's anarchist views. Madrid is under siege and their reunion is short-lived. While Ignacio works at the Pasteur Hospital in Madrid, his family searches for food during a bombardment. Death is everywhere. Battle follows battle—Belchite, Brunete, Gijón, Santander, Jarama, Teruel, Valladolid, Madrid. José Alvear returns to the Falange lines while Madrid is under siege. On a military pass to Valladolid, Ignacio, in search of Marta, discovers that she has become intensely activist and has left for Germany. In Gerona, Ignacio's mother adopts Eloy, a wandering orphan whose parents died at Guernica. Eloy becomes the first ray of sunlight penetrating Carmen Elgazu's grief since the death of César.

Access to Nationalist territory preoccupies the protagonists in the novel's last chapters. Returning to Gerona, Ignacio encounters a ski group of Nationalist infantrymen patrolling Spain's northern frontier. The peace of the Pyrenees slopes overwhelms Ignacio. Gironella in fiction here recalls his own escape over the mountains to Gerona. A poetic chapter follows. In it, Gironella describes the desperation of political factions in the last days of the war. "Fanaticism, a war to the death ... spies, living and dead heroes."[48] Franco's troops push forward into Catalonia. Gerona falls as the International Brigades are defeated and Barcelona is finally liberated. Mateo Santos is freed from prison, is united with his father, as the novel praises Franco as liberator of Barcelona: "Above all the horror, the piety, the rejoicing, and the purification, one feeling imposed itself more than any other over all the rest—veneration for the figure of General Franco. For the suffering people, Franco was their savior. For the members of the Fifth Column that counted into the thousands, his halo was magically bright."[49] Communists are executed or escape into

France. A tragic reprisal of the Communists is described in Mosén Francisco's death who, with Laura Costa, daughter of an aristocrat, is smothered, walled up in a cellar brick by brick. The exodus of 500,000 "fugitives" and their problems are also discussed: "How can people understand the pain of a half million tattered foreigners forced through customs in the space of forty-eight hours?"[50] Mateo de Soria returns home to Gerona to find Pilar Alvear and his sister Marta, the new leader of the Falange's Social Auxiliary. The entire Alvear family, with Ignacio, attends public mass, the first in three years to be held in Gerona's cathedral.

The last three chapters of *One Million Dead* evaluate the closing events of the war, and the specter of death persists despite the end of hostilities. "From time to time, a shot was heard. It was a suicide. Someone who was too sick or someone, while gazing fixedly at the Pyrenees, felt it would be too difficult to face so much uncertainty after crossing."[51] The fall of Catalonia signifies the *coup de grâce* to Communist opposition in Spain and stresses Catalonia's role as a key province of the Civil War. Gironella exonerates Catalonia from all responsibility. "None of us is responsible for what happened. Hear me! What any of us did individually, didn't count."[52] Gironella contends that the foreign press distorts the realities of the Civil War, viewing it as an international battlefield in preparation for the real arena—World War II. "Don't lose sight of one fact: the war was essentially a Spanish war. The mountain of corpses is Spanish. Don't forget it! At one predetermined moment, there were one million Spaniards fighting on the front at the battle of Teruel and twenty-five million in the rear. The international armies, all tallied, were but a drop of water in the sea."[53]

Over the radio, Franco announces the defeat of the Communist armies in the last chapter of *One Million Dead*. Thus, Gironella concludes his second volume, with Franco as the hope of Spain, without eulogy of the past or direct propaganda for the future. Despite the title, only *one* death has any consequence—that of César Alvear.

The account of the Alvear family centers upon its new member, Eloy, one of the many new characters of the third volume of the trilogy, *The Peace Has Broken Out*. Gironella declares his intention of extending the trilogy to seven or eight volumes to

document the postwar years vividly, utilizing the same method-
ology and characters.[54] Of course, Gironella runs the risk of
cheapening the quality of his earlier works.

III   *Critical Appraisal of* One Million Dead

Even more ambitious than its predecessor, *One Million Dead*
has potent reasons for success because it so broadens the base
upon which rests *The Cypresses Believe in God.* It expands upon
each of the Alvears; it extends the geographical focus of *The
Cypresses* beyond Gerona to all Spain; it relates from a panoramic perspective, sociological, political, religious, and military
conflicts of Communists and Falange simultaneously, and it
unfolds the drama of a nation in the throes of civil strife as
impartially as political conditions permit. Still, Gironella was
successful on the historical level but not necessarily on the fictional one since his *a priori* judgments of Communist personages
—Teo, Dr. Relkin, Gorki, Cosme Vila—as sadists, gangsters of a
villainous cause, are unrealistic in contrast to the heroics of the
Falangists. The Alvears, not committed politically for almost two
thousand pages, must subscribe to the Falange Party since the
connections of the family are all Falangists. In a recent review
of the novel, José Luis Cano summarizes his views of the political
aspects of *One Million Dead*:

To my surprise, in *One Million Dead,* Gironella has said, if not all
the truth about the Spanish Civil War . . . , some truths that, for the
first time are being said publicly and in a book in Spain. I refer to
the excesses of repression in the Nationalist zone, which, if they were
known and if they had been widely spoken about, Franco censorship
would have stopped its dissemination even today in works such as
these. . . . It is more logical to suppose that the book lends authority
to actual events because in its chamber of horrors about the Civil
War, Gironella lingers much more slowly on the terrors of the Communist zone and also because of his story, the figure of Franco surges
forth with the halo of a military genius comparable to Wellington
or Napoleon.[55]

Vásquez Dodero also poses an interesting theory. *Los Episodios
nacionales* (*The National Episodes*) of Pérez Galdós consider
the Spanish Revolution of 1808 the result of anti-progress and
Gironella, who tries to surpass Galdós, believes war a *fruto de*

pecado (product of sin). Galdós is far more realistic than Giro-nella but both equally attempt to perpetuate the glory of Spain. "I am sorry to say that, in my opinion, Gironella, a noble spirit, bursting with pure intentions is neither impartial (although he may have tried to be) nor rigorous in his portrayal of historical truths in the course of the novel."[56] R. M. Hornedo's commentary should be considered also an appraisal of merit, even though Gironella's original intentions for *One Million Dead* were not adhered to:

Gironella, with uncommon narrative gifts, by means of a skillful assembly of chronicles and characters of fiction, has written a tense, fictionalized report in an anti-war tone without either the story values of *All's Quiet on the Western Front* or the sparse objectivity and drama when the category of war themes and the Spanish Revo-lution, so fecund in heroism, was pressing for the greatness of epic models in one of several historical novels . . .

Neither is *One Million Dead* the religious novel that it could have been nor was it what the author had intended to write on this theme. Within the trilogy, this novel is inferior to *The Cypresses Believe in God*—once again, "sequels are ever as good as the originals"—and above all, it is a long way from being the long-awaited answer to Bernanos, Malraux, Hemingway, Koestler and Barea. But given the enormous difficulty of such a thorny theme, *in magnis et voluisse sat est* (it is enough just to have wished for great things [from his novel]).[57]

Shortly after publication of the novel, Gironella produced an autocritique, "Así escribí *Un millón muertos*" (In This Way I Wrote *One Million Dead*),[58] on the meaning of this novel and how it fulfills his stated intentions. "I wanted to write a sym-phonic novel which would bear out certain truthful events, artistically changing them and creating suitable human beings, characters that seemed to me and to my family like members of real Spanish families who experienced the Civil War."[59] A youth-ful witness to hostilities, Gironella felt he had to justify the rea-sons for the war.[60] After his first two novels and a careful study of Galdós and Pío Baroja, Gironella noted that their literary ability was weakened by lack of organization. Profiting from this discovery, he began *The Cypresses* whose genesis occurred to him one day in 1937 on the peaceful slopes of the Pyrenees.[61] Gironella explains his serious purpose. "My goal was to obtain a well-balanced work. So I put myself on guard when I wrote with easy inspiration or with excessive enthusiasm. I felt myself infinitely distant from that vain and garrulous young boy who had written *Where the Soil Was Shallow* in Baroja's style and *The Tide* without ever having set foot in Germany."[62] Before *One Million*, Gironella visited each province where major battles were fought in order to acquaint himself with the locale, the very stones, the cemeteries and their silent observers, the tall cypresses around them. "Twenty-nine million men and an entire countryside informed me of the deaths of one million men."[63]

The attempt to capture provincial flavor is a failure as is differentiation of characters. Each in its own way is weakened by what Gironella defines as "the inevitable truth,"[64] so that autobiographical experiences and characters inspired by real people never achieve a true objective existence. Gironella's war novels, thus, show little psychological perspicacity. It is this interest in laying bare the significance of the Civil War that causes this "sameness" in settings and personages. "My objective was to find out what the war was like in each place and its significance for every man."[65] Gironella makes a few attempts to dramatize characters or events but keeps narrative constantly moving in lucid prose. "Gironella's prose lacks magic and charm but it is effective as narration and as a vehicle of expression of a genuine writer— genuine for his intuitive capacity and powers of observation, for his talent to handle the several threads of the narrative and the articulation between them, for his gifts of invention of character and for sustaining interest."[66] Vásquez Dodero's comment is a pertinent documentation of the truth of Gironella's original intention: "My purpose was to imitate life under the moon and the inconstant sun, its slow tempo with sporadic tremblings...."[67] Consequently, his characters are neither exaggerations nor folkloric Spanish stereotypes. "I must transcribe the external things as well as the interior life of human beings."[68]

One Million Dead abounds in excellent exterior descriptions. The battle scenes are masterful in details of strategy and combat. The novel is less successful in the portrayal of interior life. Gironella prefers that interior monologue and dialogue alone reveal characters who are often pale types, colorless and without individuality. His predilection for the external did not allow him to adjust his perspective to grasp individual idiosyncrasies and

dimensions of feeling and understanding. His impersonality and
neutrality of spirit disallow empathy and, consequently, penetration of an interior world. Although Gironella believed the major
flaw of *One Million Dead* was "tone" and "synchronization" of
events with action, his isolation from interiority is far more serious.

The Cypresses Believe in God is certainly more poetic and
artfully written. *One Million Dead*, on the other hand, is the
more systematically organized and analytical. *The Cypresses* may
be considered as a fictional work with historical pretensions, but
One Million Dead is essentially an historical study overlaid with
fiction. *One Million Dead* is hardly what Gironella desired. Its
lack of vitality prevents it from being a commemoration, an
evocation for Spain of the unforgettable past, a voice eloquently
speaking to generations still to come.

CHAPTER 6

Illness and Preoccupations

I *Background of* Los fantasmas de mi cerebro
(Phantoms of My Brain)

AFTER *One Million Dead,* José María Gironella suffered a nervous breakdown which he called *la extraña enfermedad* ("a strange illness"),[1] and described graphically as *el túnel negro* ("the black tunnel").[2] Because of his inability to concentrate on writing the conclusion of *One Million Dead,* he turned to description of the symptoms of his breakdown and the universality of his preoccupations. He wrote some eight thousand pages about the specters which inhabited his psyche, the best of which appear in *Los fantasmas de mi cerebro* (*Phantoms of My Brain*).

The section dealing with the period of Gironella's illness is impressive in the amount of work produced. He justifies his output: "The absence of health, the impossibility of concentrating because of vertigo, the confusion in my mind due to a nervous depression and an often unexplainable tiredness frustrated my work day after day. Also the exacerbated fear of not perceiving something valuable or necessary to write about, of the increasing, unending mountain of pages to be written depressed me uselessly."[3] Gironella spent much of his work day in this period editing and provided his publishers with a definitive version of *One Million Dead. Phantoms* served as psychological therapy. Originally, Gironella planned five works but only completed half of his projects. *Phantoms, We Are All Fugitives* and newspaper articles and essays published in *ABC* and the *Diario de Barcelona* are the total result.

After publication of *Phantoms of My Brain,* Gironella explains the lack of spiritual unity in the work as a result of his illness. Without chronological unity as well, the four sections have emotional harmony in their consistent feeling of overwhelming sadness. In another "indispensable clarification," Gironella writes that his illness consisted of a nervous depression associated with an anxiety syndrome, that a series of revealing texts describe in detail his period of mental crisis, and refers to his statement to the newspapers about his illness during recuperation. His three years of "hallucinated suffering" had such relevance to doctors and laymen that he decided to set down an exhaustive inventory of its stages. He seeks to clarify his symptoms by describing them. He stresses the role of the novelist to science. His artistry serves to make psychological phenomena comprehensible. His illness demonstrates his awareness that Spain had altered spiritually since the Civil War and that new problems had arisen. Gironella uses his illness to educate members of his generation. Because his breakdown was so nearly complete, Gironella had lost all sense of shame and embarrassment in reporting his feelings. No longer responsive to societal pressures, he wrote about his feelings spontaneously, avoiding psychological nomenclature and clichés. He does not exaggerate his hallucinations nor subject them to artistic transpositions. To discover the significance of his anguish ("Anxiety belongs to a dimension that has nothing to do with language"),[4] he concentrates on relations of *symptomata* through a new dimension of perception.

II *Structure and Critical Analysis*

Phantoms of My Brain has two parts. The first is a lecture based upon his experiences presented at the University of Paris in 1957. The second, of five subsections, consists of notes written during his illness, each independent and organized according to subject matter. They show stages of his thought. The second part, chronologically and logically, precedes the first, the formal university lecture.

The first two subsections contain descriptions of preliminary symptoms. The third deals with his hallucinations; the fourth, written during recuperation, contains intimate thoughts of his home and Mallorca. The fifth and last deals with Paris. Each subsection is thematically distinct, although each thought is a unity, a sensitive and poetic revelation of the writer.

His first notes show failure of concentration, fear of leaving home, spells of vertigo, preferences for night over day, symbols of weather conditions. Paradoxically he imagines himself to be

88

under constant scrutiny. Helpless but able to report symptoms
accurately, *Phantoms* makes startling reading. Through self-
analysis, Gironella realized the "porosity" of his own feelings.
His states of depression cause him to lie, grossly and often. He
experiences alternate states of superb mental clarity and total
loss (inundation within himself). This he calls the "grey elephant
that weakens my brain."[5] His condition results in irrational statements: "At times, it seemed to me that that man was God."[6] ". . .
he absolutely believed the moon and the sea loved each other."[7]
The author is aware he has lost self-control: "Now I have no
appetite and I go on being a slave. I am a slave of my inhibition
and I suffer more than ever."[8] He suffers intensely from a feeling
of solitude: "I am not outside of things nor am I facing them. At
this moment, I am loneliness itself. I am not a drop of water
expelled from the sea; I *am* the sea."[9] The immensity of his
solitude is a surrealistic vision. His lips are beaches of the sea
with ocean spume issuing from his mouth. The sea envelops him
and he drowns.

Such experiences alternate total loss of spirit with conscious-
ness of enormous power, and delusions of grandeur: "I imagined
myself the creator of marvelous goals which were laid at the feet
of the multitudes. However, this multitude suddenly identified
me and pursued me."[10] His perception of nature is distorted or
transposed when he perceives ". . . eleven red and white under-
shirts hanging from a wire, drying . . ."[11] as the spirits of eleven
hanged men. Gironella's fascination with material objects, his
correlation of their use with the expression of his own ego is
marked: "I could even pierce myself in the brain; and immediately, millions of needles that sleep in the cerebrum raise themselves up dancing, making me suffer more and more."[12]

One of the writer's principal anxieties is escape, flight, retreat
into solitude. He seeks the significance of his marriage and
answers to fundamental questions. He believes his desire for
greatness and for popularity caused his breakdown and that his
present pain is frustration. As consolation, he smokes, his pre-
requisite for premeditated evil acts. Sleep, however, allows a
temporary escape from the realization that physically and spiritually he is slowly dying: "In the deepest part of myself, there is
a cemetery where everything stops and apparently dies."[13]

Religion and love are sustaining features in his life. Even his dream episodes of triumph and self-imposed martyrdom reflect poetically his delusions. He imagines himself to be "a phosphorescent fish,"[14] wallowing in pride and egotism. Gironella defines his illness in a lucid and revealing commentary:

I am a mental depressive . . . a man with one hundred hearts, suffering . . . a man who believed his adjectives were tigers and now understands they were flies. Son of an affectionate yet unstable father and a strong mother who was always on the defensive, I also had four brothers, each one different and distant. I was born in a small, lonely town lashed by the wind. I suffered in a seminary because a naked light bulb danced before my eyebrows. I suffered when love awakened within me because I wasn't prepared for it. I suffered in the war because at the age of eighteen, I was asked to pass sentence on soldiers and kill. I understood nothing of what occurred or its value. Incapable of imagining nothingness and satisfied only with attaining the absolute, I was condemned to float between these two extremes. . . . I have the constant feeling that a red ant enters in one ear and goes out the other . . .[15]

This is Gironella's most coherent, revealing definition of himself. He sometimes appears disingenuous, but this statement is truthful and the result of a psychological breakthrough because of his illness. His notes, episodic in nature, however, begin coherently, to become increasingly incoherent. At last, totally lacking in objectivity, they suddenly change stylistically, becoming lucid once more. The less cryptic the observation, the more impersonal the description. Better exterior descriptions indicating sustained lucidity are evidences of return to better mental health. The last section, Paris, is the most impersonal, the most descriptive, and the most coherent of the group.

Specifically, the second subsection, short attempts to explain symptoms poetically and longer prose statements, are thoughts of the past written during his illness without connections between them. They serve as clues to Gironella and his opinions. "I passed some civil guards who greeted me. 'Why don't they carry out their duties?' I thought. 'If I steal a bicycle, they would stop me; I shattered the life of so many people around me and they let me go free.'"[16]

Gironella always considered himself too young to fight, not understanding the real reasons for the war and too immature at eighteen to comprehend them. Thus, he concentrates upon himself, often at a level of childish simplicity. When asked why he likes swimming pools, he answers "because the water is green in all swimming pools and at the bottom of the pool, we kiss each other."[17] Puerile yet plausible, Gironella's commentaries cover a wide range of symptoms. Sad, in pain and conscious of his supple body, he is aware of the affective values of certain words: "Even the word 'vertigo' måkes me dizzy."[18] Life's monotony also affects him when he declares that "life is as monotonous as the teeth of a comb."[19]

Gironella is convinced that one of his mother's cancerous ovaries is exactly his own age, that cancer entered her body the night he was conceived, and that "he who kisses or plants a tree doesn't know if he's doing good or evil."[20]

"Without a doubt I am the product of a small astral trembling."[21] His depression to him is on a "cosmic" level: "Perhaps the cause of my depression was a ball of fire floating through the galaxies during the millenium. . . ."[22] His illness alienates him from society and Gironella defensively emphasizes his superiority as a consequence. Craving to be cured as quickly as possible, he prays to Christ for help. "If only Christ would take it, if He would gather up this eternal pain and transform it spiritually into happiness. . . ."[23] His longing to be cured leads him to make vain religious promises. His desperation reaches such intensity that he cries out, if God does not help him, he will no longer write. Part of the author's treatment was therapy by electric shock and he recalls the sights, sounds, sensations of this method. At times, he feels rats chew his heart. His perspective immediately shifts radically from total involvement to a clear, detached perception of the exterior world. Although his doctors tell him he shows no schizoid tendencies, Gironella's pattern of behavior is at least inconsistent.

Still, a text of this period, written with great psychological coherence, attempts to reveal his depression through biological perspective:

My parents were my first relatives and they caused in me a periodic feeling of emotional instability. My infancy was spiritually isolated because of my temperament. . . . Upon discovering the world, I injured myself excessively. . . . My five brothers and I were not united then as we are now. I lived for many years harassed by intensely religious scruples, which fought against my exuberant nature. The war encroached upon me at a crucial moment and I saw buildings and knowledge destroyed. Later I united with a woman of melancholy temperament with a smile oftentimes skeptical, which left a deep and vital impression upon me. However, there is an infinite number of other men who have shared similar experiences and continue loving and laughing.[24]

He is a composite of many personality types but cannot discern the causes for his depression.

The *noche y día* (night and day) sections may be equated respectively with unhealthful and healthful mental states. At evening, he is fearful and at the mercy of the phantom of death. Sleep prevents the author from committing suicide, yet it also provides him with absence of pain, even moments of euphoria. To his poetic descriptions of the meaning of night ("In countries honored by the sun, the night is a star. In countries where there is fog, night is a drunkard embracing a street lamp. In snow-covered countries, night is a train or an idea that crosses the plains whistling"),[25] he adds a highly personal cosmological significance. God directs the stars while man rests. The night belongs to God Who envelops the firmament. Nights are "horizontal," rest and dreams; and "vertical," study and prayer. His personal view of night results from his reactions to climate. "Frozen" nights indicate a violent break with interior coherence. "Warm" nights are smoothly integrated mental and physical harmony between himself and the universe. Night is also a personal void in which he is forced, through electro-shock treatments, to plumb the depths of his conscience, always with the same question, "Why do I exist?"

Dogs float in the air, coffins contain mail boxes for letters to reach the dead and objects dream. Still, he realizes his illness and its cure is, ultimately, his own responsibility. For everyone, one crucial night brings illumination so intense that transfiguration of body and spirit takes place. Seeking a more concrete view of life, he describes the familiar, daily phases of existence rooted in home and city which he previously had taken for granted.

As the author walks through city streets to familiarize himself with partially remembered sights, smells and objects, what he sees fatigues him for he cannot escape pertinent thoughts about his illness, his injections, antidepressant herbs and, above all, his violent reactions to electric shock. This multiplicity shows the wide-ranging impressions of the writer's vision while undergoing his cure.

All his impressions are intensely personal. His recollections of the Balearic Islands are a good example. Not as tranquil beauty, they obsess him negatively. Ibiza, island of schizophrenics, funereal Minorca whose citizens walk in black, and sad Mallorca, haven for suicides, all contradict for him the popular belief that the Balearics are a seat of paradisal happiness.

This period of recuperation, of sun bathing and of physical gratification, demonstrates Gironella's self-involvement. He analyzes his negations resulting from electric shock, the clatter of trolleys, the inexplicable need to urinate, the meaning of tears. He concentrates on explaining the inexplicable. Unimpressed by cities, he seeks escape from neon, confetti and chatter, from all the whirlwind of cities. Bookstores, museums, churches produce a dizziness impeding elevation of his spirit. Mentally, emotionally and intellectually exhausted, Gironella withdraws, and, like the heroes of his novels, repeatedly visits cemeteries to pray for strength to endure his suffering.

In Paris and with his wife, the negative sensations of the Balearics disappear and his cure is imminent. His writing is more lucid, with references less enigmatic, and he can describe exterior events impersonally. His first impressions of Paris, of its cats, of the faces staring from French doors, of the vendors scurrying to their stalls, of the endless bustle of Paris, contribute to inspire him. From death, the city of Paris awakens him to life, a satisfaction to Gironella's indefatigable curiosity. Always at the precipice of solitude, Paris helps him to realize his vitality and inspiration (as it did in the past) to continue writing. The positive nature of his experiences and genuine love which Gironella feels for Paris restored him to health.

Gironella's prose flows smoothly, but content varies. Some incidents are of vital interest while others are disjointed or dull. A homosexual's advances cause Gironella to doubt the validity of his earlier sexual preferences. His acquaintance with the mentally depressed and their *cafard* or "blues" plays on his sensitivity and sympathy without shattering his new-found strength. Gironella no longer broods about death, suicide, or his nostalgia for Spain. Apart from Spanish expatriates, he seeks a community of scholars at the University of Paris and signs a contract with his publishers to write a new novel. After a brief separation from his wife, he realizes his illness is lessening. "It frightened her that absolutely nothing would hurt me."[26] He sets out to conquer Paris and publishes the case history of his illness with the excuse that he will help others similarly afflicted. These latter notes are highly repetitious, chiefly remarks to indicate Gironella's empathy with others mentally depressed. "Life is here, close to the skin; it is absolutely necessary to be alive and love life."[27] The writing of *One Million Dead* and a study of yoga are his aids for the struggle of life day to day. These notes are valuable because of their accurate biographical information.

During this period, Gironella decided to write a collection of short stories with the major theme of escape. In fact, this theme is a fundamental reason for *Phantoms of My Brain*: "I wrote about Paris to flee the abundance of tears that came to my eyes. And all of my reflections fled from the specter of death."[28]

Phantoms has been called a "miscellaneous volume that is, at the same time, a bit autobiographical."[29] Any treatment of the work must be selective, emphasizing elements of more insight into the author, his life, his illness, and his creativity. These notes show clearly that Gironella did regain his ability to appreciate life and with a new and more profound awareness. "I began to write with feelings of love. From that moment on, a great change occurred in my inner being."[30]

The first part of the work, his lecture delivered at the University of Paris, indicates Gironella's personal selection of relevant experiences and willingness to share his former psychological anxiety with his public, but lacks the spontaneity of the acute perception in the notes themselves. It is only a highly organized prose correlation, full of clichés, and has lost much of the honesty and vitality of its original sources. Some critics consider *Phantoms of My Brain* a falsification written during a lull in his career. Nevertheless, Gironella's new interest in scientific phenomena and psychology comes as a direct result of his attempt at self-analysis.

III   *Miscellaneous Short Stories and Essays*

Gironella's illness concludes in his decision to cultivate the short story. His first piece of imaginative literature written after his illness is a fantasy based upon Giovanni Papini, the Italian religious philosopher and entitled "Muerte y juicio de Giovanni Papini" ("Death and Judgment of Giovanni Papini"). Gironella no longer uses realistic prose to rein his imagination. Stirred himself to violent melancholy by his own phantoms, in a simple, diaphanous prose he attempts to show how the imagination, properly used, can open unsuspected worlds. Gironella wrote this short story with two purposes in mind: he wanted to explain the nature of death and to pay tribute to Papini.

Death is a dense and "formidable presence" floating in a neutral kingdom, the basis of all creation and future revelation. Gironella describes Papini's journey after death and his eventual judgment in a world similar to purgatory in which Jesus, the angels, and Lucifer intermingle. This world tests Gironella's theories and doubts concerning the final judgment, transubstantiation, love, glory, and the meaning of religion. Papini faces judgment before Jesus and the devil, and his acceptance into heaven is inevitable, as is, necessarily, Gironella's concept of Christian values. The story is didactic as it traces Papini's thoughts—from intellectual nonbelief to religious convert with a possibility for future absolution and attaining to Christ. The theme of all Papini's monologues is God and His power. Gironella's hero asks the same question as Christ on the cross, repeated by Miguel de Unamuno's hero in the short story "San Manuel Bueno, Mártir" ("St. Emmanuel The Good, Martyr"): "Father, why have you forsaken me?"[31] but with a basic difference. Where Don Manuel represents the Unamunian idea that reason annihilates faith, Papini reverses, for Christ and the devil argue a rational case to win Papini. The protagonist's rational choice is Christ and salvation, or the devil and damnation.

In a brief appended essay, Gironella recalls his youthful impressions while reading Papini's *History of Christ*, and sets forth his own religious theories. For Gironella, belief in a Christ made to his own measure rests upon faith. Any sin is natural and never beyond redemption. Papini's *History of Christ* and *History of Saint Augustine* are the key works to determine Gironella's religious ideas. Gironella recalls how he read Papini's evocative prose to dispel the fears from his childhood. "Death and Judgment of Giovanni Papini" gained him an invitation to visit the philosopher's home in Florence, and his experiences there comprise his article "Con la familia de Papini en Florencia" ("With Papini's Family in Florence").

This essay contains Gironella's impressions after reading Papini's letters, his visit to Papini's widow and to his tomb. The essay is a homage to his spiritual father. Fascinated by this intimate revelation, personal memorabilia, and tape recordings of his voice, Gironella believes he profited from his visit to Florence. Originally, he intended to write a biography, unpublished as yet, of Papini (whose photograph he keeps on his mantle at his home in Arenys de Mar).[32] His documentation of the problems encountered gives significance to this essay.

Gironella summarizes his conclusions on Papini, life-death, and himself in a short, imaginative monologue entitled "Carta de un gusano a Jesucristo" ("Letter from a Worm to Jesus Christ") wherein a worm desires death and peace instead of life and continual suffering. He seeks the clemency of Jesus as well as his love: "To know that love exists and to feel myself incapable of loving...."[33] The worm seeks to transcend earth, begging Jesus for salvation and immortality. The letter is a plea for salvation for all, even the smallest creatures of the universe.

The short story about Papini is heavy-handed, but the worm's monologue is a less serious and more imaginative work for Gironella's form of pantheism. It is written with much fervor, directness, originality, and humor and reveals Gironella in a new aspect. "Letter from a Worm to Jesus Christ" is his first genuinely entertaining story to show his ability in limited subjects treated with high stylization.

His other writings of this period, many newspaper articles, his *Meditaciones* (*Meditations*), evaluate a variety of subjects, and are a microcosm of all essential thought patterns. *Meditations* agrees with the tenor of the disconnected thoughts of *Phantoms* and are usually autobiographical. The beach, the author's birthday, views of northern Europe, suicide, doctors, and hobbies all figure in these articles.

The beach is integral to his intellectual landscape. "The beach is both soothing and a place for reflection."[34] For Gironella, the beach is youth but mortality. Death is there as an old man, dreaming there of his departed youth. The beach does not grow old, for its sands are the only place youth can play and learn the true meaning of joy.

His birthday, December 31, causes Gironella's reflection: "...
I must admit that twelve strokes of the bell signify the death of
something; because the first eleven stand for the birth of my
body and the last one, the birth of my soul."[35] Gironella feels he
is drifting "between" the years and his birthday occasions unusual
youthful, personal reminiscences. It is a cue to memory of experiences—his student days at the seminary, his military service with
the Ski Patrol in the Pyrenees and his feelings of loneliness in
Paris after his breakdown.

When Gironella returns to Spain from northern Europe, he is
fascinated by the eyes of northern peoples, their significance,
and their color. Essentially, his meditation is a contrast of Nordic
and Spanish psyches and their vision of the world. His conclusions are obvious generalities with no deeply felt revelations and
with a strong bias towards the Latin temperament. Gironella
prefers Spanish eyes: "Nordic eyes just look; Spanish eyes observe."[36] Obviously, other lands and people are interpreted in
terms of himself, a theme later to be exploited in his successful
travel books.

A psychiatric sanatorium provokes his thoughts on suicide in
general and the relation of war to suicide in particular. Since the
desire to live is nourished by wartime conditions, suicidal tendencies diminish but the peacetime period and its relaxations
increase the inclination to suicide. "To live while bombs are
falling is easy; to conquer the monotony of the soul, to get up
and out of bed each day is what is more difficult."[37] Ironically he
praises war since, potentially, it saves lives (the lives of potential
suicides). The thought is certainly bizarre and typical of Gironella's new attitude and his desire to shock his public from complacency. Edward J. Gramberg notes this tendency to division:
"One always notes his urge to surprise and to grasp for transcendence by means of a laconic phrase loaded with moral
significance."[38]

For five years he was ill, so Gironella dedicates an article to
his feelings about doctors. Originally a comparison between
young and old physicians, this delightful essay presents a unique
view of medicine. The medical art is totally dependent upon two
faculties: "... scientific machinery at the service of the human
eye."[39] To account for the factors of human frailty and differences
of perception, he concludes wittily "the first thing you have to

do to cure yourself is to convince yourself that there is absolutely nothing wrong with you!"[40] He writes for laymen and with humorous intent.

Meditations ends with an article entitled "Lenin, el ajedrez y los gatos" ("Lenin, Chess and Cats"), an exercise in biography. Chess and cats were Lenin's two great personal passions. Gironella attempts to correlate the aspects of his character in terms of these two. Lenin's gift for political strategy derives from chess as the sinuous nature of cats is mirrored in Lenin's own subtlety. An homage to Lenin, this final meditation accentuates the author's own preoccupation with the nature of greatness without acceptance of any Communist platform. Gironella's political activities and principles remain nebulous and his interest in Lenin, biographical and psychological. He seeks to ascertain the causes of the Russian's fame.

IV Conclusions

Gironella's "meditations," cogently written on a variety of themes, reflect his genuine interests and show the emergence of new phases of his talent. He has become the aesthete, the stylist of the short story. He transcends himself to discover himself anew in his talent for the short story, an artistic expression of his keen sensitivity.

In perspective, the transitional *Phantoms of My Brain* is artistic raw material whose energy of execution shows Gironella's direction for the future. His *Phantoms* indicates the variety of themes for future works (travel, science, history). It is a serious, heterogeneous, autobiographical study, as it is an experiment in writing styles (realistic, surrealistic) and genres (the essay, the short story). *Phantoms* establishes the fertility of his mind, his enormous vitality, and his growing ability to control themes unified and sustained in execution. His task is to develop a personal style and aesthetic based upon descriptive analysis of his own psychological reactions.

CHAPTER 7

The Short Story

I *Intentions and Themes*

TODOS somos fugitivos (*We Are All Fugitives*) is José María Gironella's aesthetically least successful but nevertheless most appreciated work aboard. It demonstrates his ability as artist and stylist in the short story and essay. What was suggestion in *Phantoms of My Brain,* flight or escape, is the theme for seven highly original short stories. "We are all fugitives. To flee is the law. Only God is given the power to remain where He is. To grow up is to flee towards heaven. To walk is to flee forward. To sleep is to flee from our consciences.... We would all want to flee, to displace ourselves, to cross our own frontiers in search of something never before seen like immortality."[1]

His new realm of fantasy revolves about the central theme of escape.

In these tales I have not intended to *demonstrate* anything; I simply intend to *suggest.* We are not dealing with a mathematical lesson, but on the contrary, we are trying to pull the reader out of his mathematical lethargy, from his exclusive faith that two and two are four, to shake his drowsiness and get him on his feet; and trying to pursue "fugitive" thoughts—phantoms and *fugitives*—to capture those anemic agitations which sometimes last a single instant and which we cannot retain with precision. Trying to analyze, through art, what escapes us because it is too lovely, or too sad, or too incomplete.... We are dealing with poetry, but a poetry in reverse focus.[2]

Gironella has another explanation for Fernández Cuenca: "In our world, there are many frontiers we would like to secretly cross. And there are many people, while not escaping geographically, find a way to flee from themselves. This world of material and spiritual fugitives is what I am trying to capture in my work."[3]

II *Content and Analysis of Seven Short Stories*

Structurally, *We Are All Fugitives* is in two sections, narrative and essay, with no apparent attempt at correlation. The unusual grouping of short stories with a series of essays has no significance and is doubtless the idiosyncrasy of Gironella's publisher. These short stories, however, and their real-surreal-fantastic worlds mark a real advance.

The first, "Tres platos en la mesa" ("Three Plates on the Table") or "El deseo se hace carne" ("Wishing Becomes Reality") turns on escape from solitude. A fifty-five-year-old retired mathematics teacher works daily at his blackboard solving arithmetic formulae. He lives with his ten-year-old daughter, his source of happiness. She, however, exasperates her father continually with her egocentricities, but he accepts everything and tries to remedy her fault. But, and this is the surprise, she is only a figment of imagination, embodiment of his dreams, the child that could have been, the being he created to end his loneliness.

The character of the mathematician's wife who should have given birth to the child of his dreams during their marriage appears in flashbacks of the couple's meeting, courtship, marriage and middle age, to underline the sterility destroying their happiness. After an account of thirty years, the same situation reappears. He had no wife as well as no child. The wife, too, is a fiction created to satisfy his desire for companionship and escape from solitude. Both child and wife are carefully drawn for an illusion of verisimilitude.

As the conclusion, the mathematician is alone, submerged in his loneliness, still habitually setting three places for dinner. A misty dream sequence shows the family of three talking, eating, living together harmoniously. It comes as no surprise that the mathematician too has no existence. He personifies many of those living on a lonely street. In dreams to fill an empty lot, they created the mathematician, his family, and even his house. A fictitious reality attempts to compensate for a void in life.

Gironella creates the illusion of their personal realities success-fully and then deliberately destroys each image. Gironella's conception of reality may be illusion sustaining daily life or, perhaps, even the absence of illusion.

Surrealist and in the vein of Juan Rulfo's Mexican fantasy,

Pedro Páramo, Gironella's tale is based on objective reality. He examines the transitory nature of youth and innocence, love, fertility, sterility, illusion, the values of marriage and of death to explore and to resolve loneliness.

In lucid prose, the story in its concrete detail is opposed to the demands of objective reality. Gironella transcends nationality and profession for his characters exist in the nebulous world of fantasy. They represent Everyman in the twentieth century in his recognition of, and in his fight against loneliness

"El huevo rojo" ("The Red Egg") was Gironella's first attempt at science fiction. This "red egg," a one-eyed and cancerous body with blue veins, escapes from the body of a rat in which it was engendered to discover that in a great metropolis food is hard to obtain. The cancerous egg watches from a rooftop, waiting a propitious moment to select a victim and strike. The entire population is aware of its presence. They plead for artillery, cyclotrons and Röengten rays to destroy it. Paralyzed, however, by fear of what the tumor will do, they react timidly. Meanwhile, the cancer, almost human, finds in cemeteries proof of its power. The red egg pays no attention to an appeal by the city's school children. Consequently, everyone flees the city in fear. A scientist, believing it better science to capture the cancer alive, decides to call off an Air Force maneuver to destroy the egg. For nourishment the red egg attacks its first human victim since only through death can the cancer perpetuate itself. It selects a determined enemy and most robust specimen—the talented Chief Resident Surgeon of the City Hospital. As the doctor surgically removes a tumor from one patient, the cancer steals into the doctor's right shoe, springs up and into his throat, then circulates through his entire body. The surgeon, who felt only a shudder, did not suspect that the disease he worked with daily would be his fate. He became a victim of an irony as bitter as it was cruel.

This experimental science fiction story places emphasis on cancer as an instrument of death rather than on the motif of flight. If avoiding confrontation with truths, especially medical ones, is a sign of weakness or moral cowardice, escape, the natural consequence of fear, engenders monsters and an unimaginable world. Death is a reality to be faced and accepted, for it is inescapable, inevitable in life.

"Milagro en el pueblo" ("Miracle in the Town") represents

the author's commentary on the whims of nature. A prank played by nature upon two human beings is the story of Teodoro and Diana and their simultaneous birth. Teodoro, sixty-five when he is born, grows ever younger, contrary to natural laws, and witnesses Diana, from her infant days to age sixty-five and her normal nature. Both are fugitives from time. Diana's transition from infancy, childhood and old age, follows a regular progression, exactly the reverse of Teodoro's life pattern. Their mutual fascination with each other's personality is explained by the fact that they were born exactly at the same moment and in the same town. Teodoro, a watchmaker, continually measures time as he gains in energy, becoming ever younger. A grandfather-grand-daughter relationship gradually evolves into that of father-daughter, later to become a liaison when each recognizes their mutual love and they decide to marry. In five years, a gradual change in their lives has become apparent. Now they become mother-son, to terminate as grandmother-grandson.

As he grows younger, Teodoro is no longer interested in fossils as he was in his adult years, but prefers sports magazines. In Diana, the maternal instinct awakens. A reversal of roles comes to each character because of the continuous retrogression of age in Diana. When she realizes Teodoro's days are numbered since he began to assume the fetal position, Diana accepts him and his reversal. Born simultaneously, both die at precisely the same moment. "At the moment Diana entered the coffin, Teodoro, at the end of an anguished and ferocious struggle, his flesh blue from the cold, proceeded to reenter the abdomen of his pregnant mother."[4]

To believe the "miracle," one must accept Gironella's premise —an old man and a baby are born simultaneously. Gironella's intention is not to demonstrate the rarity of such phenomena but to examine one concept—the meaning and significance of time. Gironella believes man is obsessed with the concept of time and that mummification is the only method of preservation. The order and measure of time creates personality problems but the story overflows with symbolic descriptions of clocks and hourglasses. In fact, when Teodoro and Diana decide to marry, Teodoro's gift to Diana is unique—a watch set with one million rubies, whose raised cover is a mirror.

When Teodoro and Diana reach an identical chronological age

at the moment of their marriage, time stops symbolically and romantically. They journey to the symbolic source of life, the seashore, to spend their honeymoon, and from the sea Teodoro had collected his specimens of fossil fish. Teodoro's mania to collect fossils suggests that he seeks permanence in time through static material objects. Unfortunately, the author's concentration on the progression and inversion of chronological time provides the story with a conventional, predictable conclusion. Gironella began with a fairly simple idea, accurately describing the characteristics of youth and old age. Yet Gironella's sense of the reality in a world of fantasy and his compact style make of this miracle, if not a totally believable, a well written short story.

"Ryki, pájaro rey" ("Ryki, Bird-King") is dedicated to Walt Disney, whose fantastic anthropomorphic caricatures dwell in a world in which Ryki could certainly participate. Ryki is a playful thrush-like bird whose excuse for existence is happiness. One day hunters invade Ryki's sanctuary in search of game. Ryki is forced to flee from guns and the sight of his dead fellow creatures. With earth no longer a refuge, Ryki plunges into a nearby sea, defying his anatomy. Surprisingly, he survives under these new conditions. In this alien, aquatic society, fish, its inhabitants, are astounded by Ryki's adaptation. Ryki learns to understand and to communicate with his new-found friends. He is proclaimed Bird-King of the Sea and rules his new world. His fellow sea creatures all pay him homage at a festival in his honor. At the festival, Ryki sings and charms his new-found subjects with his "earthly" talents. They offer themselves as guides to the entire ocean world. Ryki refuses because he cannot swim. This is Gironella's reminder that physical reality, nature, is inescapable. Nevertheless, a jelly-fish loves the Bird-King of the Sea, crying for him constantly, believing Ryki's destiny Messianic. Ryki finally travels to the waters surrounding Japan. The sea heaves violently and an atomic explosion casts Ryki on a burning, volcanic heap. His aquatic companions die for they are unable to adapt to breathing air. His feathers and wings burned by the force of the explosion, Ryki seeks shelter and, surprisingly, chooses an open oyster which closes over him in receding waters filled with boiling bubbles, dead fish and radioactivity.

Ryki represents man's eternal search for happiness, which even his naturally happy disposition cannot insure. Gironella reveals that Ryki's tragedy results from a failure to cope with society as it is and the consequences of escape. He stresses the instinct for self-preservation and somewhat fantastically suggests there is nothing for Ryki except his own nature. Ryki's tragic error is that the oyster, a friendly creature in the sea, is no refuge in a landscape atomically blasted. Ryki *erroneously* mistakes the relevance of the oyster to his need. This error may be attributed to egotism, or to his attempt to overcome mortality. Ironically, because of his lack of judgment, he only succeeds in destroying himself.

"El Goya y las montañas" ("Goya and the Mountains") describes Gironella's attitude towards reality. Mondariz, a poor house painter whose nickname is Goya, after his fall from a scaffold turns to painting and, aware that the artist's task is to transform reality, creates his illusions with "everlasting" paint. He delights his infirm wife, who believes in their reality. To overcome his wife's melancholy, Goya paints a masterpiece—the son the couple could not have naturally. His wife's tubercular condition is responsible for his second great work. A doctor had prescribed at least two years in a dry mountain climate. Once more a creative artist, "Goya" transposes reality. He paints on his wife's bosom a mountain setting of snow, trees, dry air. Having "set the scene," he asks his wife to breathe deeply while viewing the "live" painting in a mirror. Her lungs wheezed, but now she breathes easily.

Although this short story, like "Ryki, Bird-King," has no philosophical value, its message is equally appealing. Gironella indicates another path by which to escape the realities of illness and/or sterility: substitution. The meaning is transparent. The true function of the artist is to recreate a world entire. As Goya y Lucientes' evocative etchings and oils in his imagination intensified the realities of the court of Charles IV and of the Spanish Revolution, so "Goya" creates a new world to which he and his wife may escape. The artist alone determines the value of his work.

"El suicida y su hermano" ("The Suicidal Twin and His Brother") is the story of two brothers, the Gandol twins, Benito and Amadeo, each of whom searches for his individual liberty and the expression of his individual free will. Natives of San Feliü de Guíxols, the brothers live in harmony, wholly identified with one another until Benito decides to marry. Amadeo, however, remains a bachelor and a dreamer. Unable to cope with his solitude after Benito's marriage, Amadeo's character is transformed radically. Envy burns in Amadeo's heart as he secretly wishes his sister-in-law a miscarriage. The sibling jealousy is exposed and ultimately it separates them. "You hate me, Amadeo. I noticed it a long time ago. And the worst thing is that I'm responsible. I would probably have reacted the same way myself. . . ."[5] To leave San Feliü is the only practical solution to Amadeo by which to end their fraternal rivalry. On the day of his departure, he arrives at Benito's home, bringing champagne and candy for the family. Amadeo departs after a final embrace. Realizing they are identical twins, Amadeo suspects that Benito some day would experience his own feelings and therefore, his departure might spare Benito from agony like his own. Before abandoning San Feliü, Amadeo visits the local cemetery and the graves of his parents. At that instant he decides upon suicide for he realizes his envy of Benito is ineradicable. But, several seconds before his suicide, the sound of another shot causes him to return. His brother, Benito, had killed himself.

In the emphasis on its surprising conclusion, Gironella envisages Amadeo as a fugitive from an inexplicable feeling of envy arising from the heredity of identical twins. If there is an argument, it is that man must seek his own independence, individuality and freedom, for no human being should live in the shadow of another.

"La muerte del mar" ("Death of the Sea") is the last as it is his most incredible tale. Two lighthouse keepers, Basilio and his son Félix, enjoy true community of spirit in occupation and in relation. Basilio worships his son who is to him a reflection of his own youth and with identical interests since Félix is Basilio's apprentice. Although the townspeople avoid the pair because of their unity and their refusal to join the community, the lighthouse keepers give the townsmen a feeling of security. Their lighthouse stands on the highest point and from it the most hazardous storms are visible. Their beacon is a signal, a point of reference, and daily security from the sea. The sea, for the lighthouse keepers, is security and sustenance.

Félix, on the eve of his fourteenth birthday, dreamed the sea tasted sweet and that the water turned from blue to blood red.

He awakens to wildly screaming sea gulls overhead. Rising to investigate, he stands mute beneath a sky like coagulated blood and before a receding and slowly petrifying sea. "Father, the sea is dying. . . ."[6]

Félix runs to town to tell the incredulous townspeople who at last believe him. Since the sea is the only excuse for existence of lighthouse keepers, its petrification means total loss of security and motivation for existence. Basilio and Félix cross lime and sand to find some part of the sea. Even a pool of sea water could save the sea from death.

Far out in the ocean floor, they discover an unpetrified well. The townspeople, watching from shore, know a "live" bit of sea means instantaneous death, for the pair who had walked out to a depth far beyond safety did not foresee the suction of the well. Both father and son are sacrificed to the only living sea. The townspeople grieve at their deaths while the sun, a silent spectator, observes "clear and eternal."[7]

This surrealistic tale stresses that all men are fugitives from inevitable death. In this gentle and poetic father-son relationship that merits fulfillment, Gironella juxtaposes a heavy allegorical and surrealist fiction—the sea's petrification and its destruction of the lighthouse keepers. Death symbols of blood-red sky and silent setting sun are striking images for an immediate emotional response. The story's conclusion does not explain whether the lighthouse keepers resurrected the sea. The last tale is least successful because in attempting symbols lending allegorical significance to the plot, the story pretends to be more important than it really is.

III   *Conclusions*

Through his fantasies, Gironella establishes that all men are fugitives from loneliness, disease, time, reality, heredity, death, and from each other. Each clearly written fantasy is dramatically sustained by highly original perception, and these stories, written after recovery from a nervous breakdown, indirectly indicate how the author's fantastic world of hallucinations touches upon profundity. His new-found aesthetic sense effectively creates, in the realm of the short story, a private cosmos that is undeniably Gironella's own.

CHAPTER 8

Gironella and Contemporary Spain

I Gironella's First "Modern" Novel;
Background and Content

MUJER, *levántate y anda* (*Woman, Arise and Walk*) is José María Gironella's first novel after his illness. After the hallucinatory worlds of *Phantoms of My Brain* and his exploration of the improbable in *We Are All Fugitives*, Gironella turned to the physical, emotional, and spiritual realities of contemporary Spain. He is chiefly interested in his rediscovery of Spain and its people.

Woman, then, is the author's first fictional response to psychological disturbance after recovery from his nervous breakdown. It is a poorly written and unimaginative reworking of the Faustus theme of sin and redemption. Gironella's novel was criticized adversely for "pseudo-Unamunian" thematic repetition and poor quality in general. "The author has several ideas which are repeated throughout his literary production: faith, salvation, love of one's neighbor, etc.... If *Women, Arise and Walk* had belonged to the early years of the author's career, we could have expected a change of orientation, an enrichment of theme or an improvement of his means of expression. But because this novel is the result of youthful experience (supposedly when Gironella was sixteen), it is better not to concoct any illusions. We hope that we're wrong."[1] Nevertheless, the novel's Myriam may be easily identified as the author, a first projection of his uneasy days after his illness. That the setting of the novel may be Rome is of little consequence. Myriam "... is the faithful portrait of a person whom I knew, and will never forget."[2] Spiritually expatriated, Myriam because of World War II and the author because of his participation in the Spanish Civil War, both experience intense periods of solitude interrupted only by occasional diverting ideas or neurotic crises. Both dream of suicide because of their melancholia. Consequently, to Myriam, Gironella brings everything he experienced himself in his depression.

Woman is a testing ground for a philosophical polemic in which characters present opposing points of view. Hauer, a scientist for whom his profession is the only solution to end superstition, to tap undiscovered sources of energy and touch man's poetic and imaginative nature, opposes Doctor Enmanuale, a psychiatrist and Hauer's philosophical antithesis. Both are concerned with problems and moral issues of contemporary society. For Hauer, only intellectual dilemmas are valid but Enmanuale believes that moral problems, such as that of man's solitude, are primary. His solution to the question of solitude is based on love of one's neighbor and love of God. For Hauer, love is equivalent to narcissism, egoism, the cult of the healthy, disciplined body. Hauer believes in the inevitability of death since religion's life after death only deludes and pacifies the masses. God as Prime Mover and Creator of the universe is a principle without proof. One must commit himself to total disbelief in the supernatural and in religion.

A lengthy ideological debate between these two characters in Myriam's mind has little to do with the largely mental action of the novel. Nevertheless, Myriam's psychological and therapeutic discussions with her psychiatrist give Gironella occasion to develop his own meanings of love and of God.

Myriam succumbs easily to Hauer's ideas because she is rootless, systemless, prisoner of her solitude. She intends suicide because of an affair with the German scientist, but her egocentricity and cowardice prevent her. Gironella illustrates Myriam's illness in detail (in reality a description of the deterioration of his own nervous system and a commentary upon his own therapy). "... she suffered a classic case of measles, just like the ones reported in neurological case histories and visited insane asylums as well as various medical clinics, visits about which she retained dark memories and above all, memories of those experiences having to do with depressions treated by electro-shock."[3] Myriam becomes Dr. Enmanuale's patient after his discussion of his views on psychology on a Roman television program. For Dr. Enmanuale, all mental illness has a biochemical origin and can be treated medically. Death is unavoidable and, in Unamunian fashion, greater freedom for the individual is possible after coming to grips with the idea of death. Freedom must be based on ability to perceive accurately. Triumph over inadequacies and facing fundamental problems of life give responsibility. Thereafter, the individual can seek perfection, with the concept of God as model.

Dr. Enmanuale is religious because of his daily two-hour readings in the Old Testament, an eccentric since he collects legends about lakes, and a talented artist because of his love for music. His musical sensitivity derives from his profound respect for mathematics and his feelings for nature. He is a man of action, a pragmatist and thoroughly responsible. An enemy to indifference, he is egotistical like Hauer (with whom he shares many views). Myriam is caught between the magnetism of each man's personality and the powerful expression of their ideologies. She continually assumes the fetal position and indecision makes it impossible for her to act.

Myriam's symptoms and thoughts are largely those of Gironella in *Phantoms and Fugitives.* Her eroticism, impulsive nature, apathy, lack of faith, cowardice, hidden desires, masochism, and the daily traumas resulting from her pregnancy by Hauer are revealed through nondirectional psychological therapy. In fact, it is her illicit liaison with Hauer which precipitates her nervous breakdown.

The novel has no feeling for truth when Enmanuale proceeds to analyze Hauer as a character type, the usual conception of the German scientist—vigorous, healthy, self-willed, progressive, a partisan of the strong and an enemy of the weak. When the doctor identifies Hauer as Satan, the novel assumes a pseudo-religious tone and loses artistic validity. "To believe in Satan, Myriam, I can assure you isn't a testimonial to ignorance. The point of departure is simple: belief in God. That person who believes in God is automatically qualified to believe in his natural adversary—Satan."[4]

Woman paces slowly to its conclusion, and Myriam, obsessed by the idea of salvation, evaluates her condition. Realizing her insatiable drive for pleasure and its frustration as the cause of her solitude, she discovers a new definition and meaning for love. Through the happiness of others, she understands the value of suffering and the essential values of life.

II *Critical Appraisal of* Woman, Arise and Walk

Woman is surprisingly short, with only five chapters and some 170 pages, but Gironella expands and inflates a small, small theme. Myriam repeats verbatim in part or in their entirety statements of her conversations to reemphasize their meaning. Perhaps psychological necessity may require such reiteration, but as a stylistic device it is discouraging.

At the novel's end, Myriam, a totally subjective, egotistically oriented woman, has progressed to a stronger, objective and less emotional personality. She confronts Hauer, slaps him, and finally ends their affair. This vitality has its causes, in restoring to the chaos of Myriam's world an order proceeding from faith in God, in herself and in the virtues of love. She venerates Dr. Enmanuale as a Christ. In fact, Myriam believes he *is* Christ and Hauer, the devil. She renounces her sybaritic pleasures with Hauer for an heroic but modest concept of love. Myriam cannot accept either the idea of a child or of an abortion. So, confused, she returns to Dr. Enmanuale. The melodramatic situation gives Gironella one more chance for Myriam since man is free to create his own heaven or hell. Myriam can promise to have and rear her unborn child. This she does.

Premature birth to Myriam of an infant freak, and its four weeks of life and its eventual death conclude the novel. Her care for this child was Myriam's cross for her illicit affair with Hauer and, through it, she attains salvation. Gironella offers a pseudo-religious moral novel of contemporary morals and manners that says very little of any consequence although it does seem to indicate a greater recognition of mental illness in contemporary Spanish society.

Possibly *Woman, Arise and Walk* was based on the biblical Myriam of Numbers 12:1 wherein she opposes Moses' marriage to the Ethiopian woman, becomes leprous, and is cast out of camp for seven days to bear a dead child whose flesh is half consumed when it leaves the mother's womb. Gironella remarks that a "Myriam" never existed before in Spain and that his duty was to bring her and her problems to the attention of the public.[5] *Woman* implies that such problems are widespread throughout Europe and are typical. Alienation and solitude have no national boundaries and concern many recent popular European novels and films.

III   Gironella's Contemporary Essays on Spain

Although Gironella limited himself to explore the problems of mental illness in *Woman,* he exhibits greater diversity of interests in the problems of contemporary Spain in his newspaper reporting. Gironella's newspaper articles, published in *Phantoms and Fugitives* under the collective title *Temas españoles* (*Spanish Themes*) between the years 1950-60 (originally appearing in a variety of periodicals: i.e., *ABC, Diario de Barcelona* and *Ateneo*) attest to his rediscovery of his native land, and deal with a wide and very Spanish range of themes to document his new and enlarged perspectives.

As early as 1953, José María Gironella's newspaper articles, analytical and declamatory, appealed for reform of some contemporary Spanish abuses and suggested remedies.

In his essay, "Oro en el Pirineo Catalán" ("Gold in the Catalonian Pyrenees"), based on his reminiscences, Gironella discusses the problem of refugees after the Civil War. In the Pyrenees are buried treasure, contraband, and bodies of Spaniards who, defeated, attempted unsuccessfully to flee into France. Expanding upon this theme in "Los exilados españoles y los Reyes Magos" ("Exiled Spaniards and the Magi Kings") he explores the psychology of such refugees in a vignette of a group of Spaniards who, despite exile, insist upon retaining their Spanish heritage. They continue to celebrate the traditional feast of the Epiphany, testimony to their religious fervor and national pride. The various party ideologies that separated Spaniards during the war no longer exist among these immigrants who are united in their Spanish identity. Ironically, Gironella notes that such unity could not be achieved on Spanish soil before and during the war. (These two essays on the Civil War are part of Gironella's desire to comprehend it.)

"Saber dudar" ("To Know How to Doubt") is a plain-spoken analysis of the Spanish temper, its insularity and its resistance to change. He holds that the impulsive nature of the Spaniard to decide quickly manifests itself in an historical tradition to condemn rather than to judge. "It is better to die first than set things right. . . . Upon looking, we investigate; upon smelling, we accuse."[6] If the Spaniard can learn to doubt, he may search for truth.

The Spanish spirit is subjected also to severe criticism in his

article entitled "Rutas desérticas" ("Deserted Routes"), in which
Gironella believes the true soul of Spain is to be found in provincial lands and peoples and not in such cities as Madrid or
Barcelona. Like Azorín, Gironella says all Spain's problems
emanate from the land. His prose, descriptive of the countryside,
presents his synthesis of the basic elements of what is popularly
called "the Spanish spirit" or "the Spanish soul":

A thorough trip, observing our terrain constitutes an education beyond compare. It shows great afflictions and at the same time, great
waves of love which are heartrending. The mind raises a thousand
questions and it resolves and explains another thousand at the same
time. Eyes discover castles, sharp mountain ranges, buildings the
color of mud, bell towers of incredible beauty. Accumulated riches
in unknown spots—fertile plains in places where the mind imagined
bleak plateaus, black pigs where brave bulls had been, donkeys, hundreds of donkeys where you would like to see motor-driven vehicles
and tractors. What a mixture of grandeur and misery! What extensive
horizons before small towns inhabited by our illiterate brothers! Our
surprise is continuous, unforeseeable concerning what is offered to our
view upon turning a curve or looking down from a mountaintop.[7]

Spain is always emotionally charged for him. He notes the
greater incidence of divorce in large cities and the poverty of
Spain's provinces. The lack of interest in remedying such
problems is mainly the result of the Spaniard's passivity. Lacking
curiosity, they divert their energies to sport, gambling, or conversation in the cafés in an egoistic detachment of the Spaniard
from his nation. This is responsible for his physical and mental
abulia or inertia, as it is for Spain's decadence.

In "Los niños ricos" ("Rich Children") he attacks a new class
of wealthy young men. They are a narcissistic group who worship their bodies and affect mannerisms imitated from North
American films. A cutting phrase, "beings without any mental
excitement,"[8] describes them. Gironella's condemnation of these
poolside parasites is an intense reaction resulting from his own
austere youth and its days of constant crisis.

Gironella is critical of the serious effects of the motion picture
on Spain and recognizes that his country does not produce, but
imports, films. He attributes this not to censorship under Franco
but to the Spaniard's lack of imagination. Spain has the raw
materials to create a superb film industry, but dissipates them,

just as the Spaniard daily dissipates his imaginative energies in conversation. Truly good Spanish films are few. Gironella wonders whether the Spanish government will ever aid the sensitive artist to creative film productivity and permit Spain to compete artistically and intellectually with other European nations.[9]

In the early 1950's, José María Gironella noticed the great increase in religious publications, especially pamphlets appealing to "fire and brimstone." They were ineffective, but Gironella views their increasing circulation as a part of the Spaniard's excessive religious indulgence. As he questions the motives behind publication of these pamphlets, Gironella directs his attention to religion's proper appeal. Publications like these treat of one aspect of religion only—negation of sin rather than an inspiration to fortify the Spaniard in his daily life. "Los consultarios morales" ("Moral Advice") sums up Gironella's portrait of Spanish character between 1950 and 1960. Spaniards are indulgent as they recall their Civil War experiences, clannish when they travel abroad, reactionary, apathetic, affected in affluence, wasteful, unimaginative, constantly misdirecting their energies to futile talk. Above all, they are fearful of repressive religion. From this summary, Gironella views the Spaniard as immature, uncertain of his strength, constantly wavering in direction, generally unproductive. He is divorced from the great traditions.

IV   Gironella's Essays About His European Travels

Gironella is effective when he evaluates himself and his nation for a broadening of the intellectual horizons of Spain. Spain's insularity is the essential problem that creates dogmatic thought and behavior. Therefore, Gironella resolved to enlarge his own perspectives through travel. To gain keener insights into his own nation and its problems and counteract his own mental inertia, he embarked on a European tour with his wife. Essays under the collective titles "Temas italianos" ("Italian Themes"), "Temas franceses" ("French Themes), and "Temas anglosajones" ("English Themes") published in *Phantoms* reveal in his experiences abroad his perspicacity and intelligence.

A. *Italy*

The newspaper articles entitled "Italian Themes" set the tone for his future travel books. His journey from Barcelona to Rome reveals his egotism in a chatty, conversational manner. His very visual impressions on arriving in Rome are as valid as any tourist's. Sometimes his images are confused because their great number and variety prevent logical sequence and Gironella's insecurities and pessimitic attitudes show his obvious inexperiences as a traveller. On arrival in Rome, Gironella begins to write a portrait of the great city and its people. From a study of Rome and its monuments, streets, bridges and churches, Gironella hopes to achieve a deeper knowledge of Rome and Romans. He hopes, too, to distill the essence of Italian life through visual stimuli. His morbid fascination for death appears in the article "Esquelas mortuorias en Italia" ("Death Notices in Italy").

He wrote the essay "Realidades italianas" ("Italian Realities") to repudiate Lamartine's description of Italy as a land of the dead. He asserts the Italians are progressive, blessed with the spirit of activity (the key to their existence). In "Death Notices in Italy" he discusses an Italian preoccupation with death and the differences between Italian and Spanish epitaphs, with examples. He finds the Italian personality has a double standard. In life the Italian is taciturn and unnoticed, but after death his epitaph expatiates upon his virtues.

Religion's fascination for Gironella is demonstrated in the story of his visit to the Abbey of Monte Casino which, after being totally destroyed, was reconstructed stone by stone on four separate occasions. While the author admired the Italian spirit, recognized the Italians' past dominance in art, letters, religion, politics, he noted, specifically in Rome, their indifference towards abstract ideas. He foresees Italians will continue to live in the same fashion and ". . . Rome will continue being Rome."[10]

B. *France*

The essays in "French Themes" are as revealing as they are thematically disparate, unrelated, and whimsical. A tour of the catacombs of Paris is Gironella's point of departure for commentaries on his fellow international tourists, reflections on life and death, the life cycle viewed as the extinguishing of a burning candle, and his amazement at the sight of a single skull.

Gironella accurately describes the buildings, inhabitants, role and peculiarities of groups at the University of Paris. For the international pavilions, a meal in the cafeteria of the International House is one of the most common experiences of student life vividly described by Gironella.

Gironella makes commenetary on political structures of France and England from a comparative point of view and demonstrates that the essay remains a popular medium even if his ideas are of no political value: "If the English Queen breaks a leg while riding a horse, many English women will cry about it; however if Monsieur Auriol breaks his leg, the French would just laugh."[11]

His interest in the White Russian community of Paris suggests a curiosity to describe the role of the immigrant in Parisian society. He seeks to comprehend Russian immigrants' resistance to European mores, praises their impermeability to Western ideas, and correlates their patriotism with the equal intensity of Spanish tradition.

Gironella has two reasons for his admiration of the French. Despite their ineffectual political strategists, the French have consistently contributed progress to the Western world. France is also unique because she always absorbs all immigrants and expatriates. Gironella is personally thankful for France's granting of political asylum because Spaniards could seek refuge there after the Civil War without fear of forced repatriation.

His impressions of a visit to a cemetery in Toulouse emphasize again the fascination cemeteries have for him. He is genuinely moved to profound melancholy before the rich Pantheons, the poor graves, the symbolic crossed hoe and hammer over the cemetery gate. Two essential implements to sustain life form the instrument of death and the Christian's hope of immortality.

In "Oratoria sagrada" ("A Sacred Oratory") Gironella acknowledges the different and pleasing nuances of French oratory. He judges the French to be more poetic than the Spanish, more inspired by love and less by terror, less spectacular but more lyrical in its foundations of Gregorian Chant.

His final essay "Conmovedora noticia" ("A Poignant Bit of News") states his thoughts during a visit to Spanish lepers at St. Louis Hospital in Paris. He writes with sympathy of their lives, their refuge, their common leprosy, of their isolation from the vibrant life of Paris.

Newspaper articles written in France dealt with a wider variety of themes than those in the Italian section. The essays themselves were written with more understanding, greater sensitivity and delicacy than the Italian articles. Tersely, Gironella discusses politics, student life, antiquities, tourism, ethnic groups, music, art, and illness. Some of these he could not have attempted on Spanish soil.

C. *England and English-Speaking Peoples*

The major emphasis of his "English Themes" is on reactions to themes not necessarily prompted by his visit. The first of these reflections, "Scotland Yard y la quiromancia" ("Scotland Yard and Palmistry"), is a tribute to this highly organized agency because of its excellent Fingerprint Bureau. He develops from this discussion the abstract concept that England itself is built upon the inscrutable and clear foundations of the logic of Scotland Yard.

"No hay por qué asustarse" ("There Is No Reason to Be Frightened") contains the author's impressions concerning the speed of life in a great modern metropolis such as London. He discusses types of transportation, the dynamic dissemination of news, and its total effect upon the daily lives of the city's inhabitants. Extending his discussion of society one step further in "El mundo no se ha vuelto loco" ("The World Hasn't Gone Mad"), he describes the variety of professions arising from its dynamism. He also defines its "hero-types": ". . . a nearly complete collection of the different types of heroism—individual, collective, spectacular, anonymous, war-like, sportsmanlike, sacred."[12] Gironella believes England attained greatness because of her synthesis of the heroic aspects of scientific, religious, and sportsmanlike attitudes.

"Una estadística sorprendente" ("A Surprising Statistic"), on the destiny of all English-speaking peoples including Americans, contains a Spaniard's judgment of American society: "They imagine that Americans are not only owners of automobiles and homes with gardens but possess powerful brains, a gift for organization and are cultured, too."[13] He approves the effectiveness of a government created for the majority and ruled by a minority, the double triumph of work and organizational principles, creation of a huge industrial production. He criticizes Americans gently, believing success at work helps them to overcome a lack of intellectual maturity. Although this commentary may be construed as anti-American, it reflects his use of faulty information and Gironella's reliance upon hearsay. He had not been in America when he wrote this essay.

"Un belén norteamericano en París" ("A North American Nativity in Paris") relates his Christmas visit to a newly-married North American couple, recent converts to Catholicism. Their crèche to celebrate Christmas astounds Gironella by its modern conceptions—its heated rooms instead of a stable in the manger, its electric trains for donkeys. Although the young couple's rationalization for these changes is their recent conversion, their modern reconstruction of Jesus' birthplace stimulates Gironella to conclude that every nation or ethnic group who subscribes to Catholicism interprets individually and nationally its conception of the Nativity. "Each country dresses its shepherdesses in available materials. Therefore, in Japan . . . the Virgin is dressed in a kimono."[14] Gironella sought the intrinsic beauty in national interpretations of Catholicism and rejected, however, the modern conceptions opposing traditional Spanish Catholicism. He prefers, for example, a Latin rather than a vernacular Mass.[15]

Returning to Gerona, Gironella took opportunity to reflect on his impressions and the state of tourism throughout Spain. Generally, he discovers that tourists are ignorant of the countries, civilizations and monuments they observe. Most foreign tourists in Spain are the *ciudadanos-masa* or the middle class. Ironically, Spain's *hombre-masa* or mass man has little opportunity for travel. Gironella repeats Azorín's "ya es tarde" ("it is already too late"), arguing the Spaniard's fatalistic view of life impedes his will. Gironella reproves growth of intellectual curiosity among Spaniards to visit other lands, emphasizing their chronic xenophobia, conformity, and insularity.

V *Conclusions*

These reflections on Spain and other European nations are valuable since they indicate changing perspectives and liberal attitudes. Exceedingly aware of the many prejudices in his own country, his last essay, "Los turistas hablan" ("The Tourists Speak Out") is Gironella's most recent attempt to bridge Spain's intellectual gulf between herself and Europe.

Like the government thirty years after the outbreak of Civil War, Gironella recognizes that new currents are changing the structure of Spanish life. Industrialization and emergence from economic isolation are transforming Spain into a modern nation. He reflects this new attitude although he complains periodically of the rigid government censorship (Gironella's writing must be approved for publication by a government censor).[16]

In his encouragement of the growth of a new generation, freed from the fears of the Civil War, Gironella's reports of his travels abroad contribute to participation in the European community.

CHAPTER 9

World Traveller

I   Gironella's First Travel Book:
Content and Evaluation of Travels in Egypt, Ceylon and India

AS EARLY as 1953, José María Gironella recognized Spain's
need for participation in the European community, increased
communication, and greater facility for foreign travel. Travelling
through Europe, the Western Hemisphere and the Orient, Gironella, through personal reports of his travel experiences, sought
to adjust the Spaniard's peninsular perspective to more international ones.

His first book dealing with this is *Personas, ideas y mares*
(*Persons, Ideas and Seas*), thoughts in diary form, published in
1963. Semifictionalized, it is a narrative of forty days aboard the
freighter "Almudena" en route to the Orient. Gironella describes
daily life, personalities of the crewmen, and his experiences of
his voyage. As an adventurer, Gironella each day begins his
report with the question, "I wonder where the "Almudena" will
take me?"[1] *Persons* becomes more than a journal and reflects
Gironella's desire to report significant experiences. He plans to
share Egypt, Ceylon, and India with his public and hopes to
achieve the love and camaraderie of the "Almudena's" crew.

As usual, he sets the tone by introducing background material.
Hacia el puerto de embarque (*To the Shipping Dock*) relates
preparations before embarkation. The first day of his journal is
dated October 15, 1962. (The entire work is systematically dated
until the author loses patience with chronology, and his last
entry, November 20, 1962, leaves at least one hundred pages
before the end of the volume.) Barcelona is drenched by rain
but Gironella leaves in the storm for Tarragona and the Orient.
The rains of his departure provide an occasion for meditation,
especially on death and its repugnance. For relief, Gironella

turns to Eugenio d'Ors's definition of the novel which he compares with his own. His thoughts, however, are random and without sequence. Since he considers *Persons, Ideas and Seas* the product of a personal confrontation with reality, he does not attempt to restrain his flow. He writes in a spirit of freedom from geographical and ideological barriers.

With side trips on his way to Tarragona, he appraises favorably Catalonia's famed architect, Antonio Gaudí. Gironella read the history and legends of Tarragona. From the beginning, he reports his reactions to newspapers and periodicals in style, in accuracy, and in content. A newspaper condemning Mahatma Ghandi for *not* being Catholic is condemned by Gironella for taking the attitude that Catholicism is the *only* road to salvation. The journal narrative has a number of Gironella's personal reactions to his own rhetorical questions: "What am I looking for on this trip? To enrich my spirit. . . . With what kind of spirit am I undertaking this trip? With my anxiety for knowledge, my personal skepticism, and my curiosity."[2]

The introductory chapter is personal, at once engaging and confusing us, for the capricious element in Gironella's style gives the impression that *Persons, Ideas and Seas* is only a series of floating thoughts of minor importance.

Although the first hundred pages of *Persons* are written in conversational tone to recall associations, they treat three themes of the journey: those people Gironella meets or expects to meet, his preoccupations and evolving ideas, his daily shipboard experiences. Gironella's thoughts in the first section turn on his future meeting with his old friend, Georges Imbert, in Port Said.

The entire crew of the "Almudena" is sketched in short, concise summaries of their characters. Gironella also takes up the class system among passengers and marine designations of rank. His conversations with passengers and crew make this chapter. His wife is hardly mentioned. She is a shadowy figure who plays a peripheral role.

In Port Said, Gironella is greeted by Georges Imbert and their conversations on shipboard are the substance of the chapter. Demetrio, a steward who accords Gironella hero worship, is also a major figure. He is a native of Santander, ". . . very young, robust and made of stern stuff"[3] with an insatiable curiosity centering on Gironella, his method of writing novels and why he wrote about the Civil War. Gironella seizes an opportunity for revelations about himself and his work. Other passengers and crew are referred to only by name and without psychological insight.

Gironella's response to the sea is treated at length but as ideas they are ephemeral and defy organization. An example is explanatory. Gironella meditates as the "Almudena" departs. The day of departure is the anniversary of the deaths of Chopin and Ramón y Cajal. Gironella shares the latter's preoccupations with Spain and attitudes of greater ideological exchange: "I see here a certain narcissism, a sterile complacency in sounding off to oneself. We are a people who expound theories, chatterboxes—the very same ones Cajal wrote about in his *Café Chatter*—and we have not advanced one step to correct this defect. . . . Spain, Spain. I *don't* want this word to obsess me or to castrate me."[4] Gironella evaluates the state of contemporary letters and politics: "The poor writer is the one who limits himself to the local chronicles and to description of local tradition complete with expressive regionalisms no matter how elegantly he may write them. And the poor politician, the local *politico* is the one who thinks that the essence of the world revolves around him."[5] He cites Gregorio Marañón's concept of a classless society and believes he owes much to Nikos Kazantzakis as well. His interest in science he attributes to Jagadis Chandra Bose, a great contemporary Indian biologist who is the originator of the theory that plants and minerals have souls. Gironella, himself (like Shakespeare), believes his own immortality lies in his writing. "I want my writings to survive, to achieve world-wide immortality."[6] "I have to make a vivisection of Spain, although it may carry me into discomforting thoughts. Because after all, books last longer than politics. . . ."[7]

Later examining photographs from World War II, Gironella's opinion on Hitler, Churchill and Roosevelt indicate his own interest in politics, history, and the meaning of greatness. He notes that politics as such is never discussed on the "Almudena." In the words of Buchito, the radio operator, "Politics are like electricity—in order to succeed in it, you have to be an expert technician and, besides, you run the risk of being electrocuted."[8]

Turkey was not included in his itinerary: this causes Gironella to think about the expulsion of Sephardic Jews from Spain.

Spain would have been a world power if the Jews had remained. Similarly, because Gironella cannot visit Greece, he meditates on the Aegean Sea and mythology. There are a number of analogous pointless meditations and conversations.

When Gironella looks at the sea, he becomes introspective and muses on life, death, and his career. Nature is a dynamic force whose movement harmonizes with God. The immensity of the sea accentuates Gironella's feeling of mortality. Gironella believes he is weak and must seek redemption from cowardice and dishonesty through war and death. He remembers Ortega y Gasset's view of the futility of war, and repudiates Communist ideology as a philosophy which negates all that is natural and typical. He echoes Unamuno in his pronouncement of man's tragic sentiment, that fatalism impedes the individual from reconciliation with faith. He places mistrust in Gregorio Marañón's writings and their organic conception. We are certain of life while we live and, parodoxically, we die each day.

Gironella responds fatalistically to the banks of the Suez as the "Almudena" passes through its locks. The coast of Egypt induces a long discussion of tombs, burial ceremonies, mummification, and the Egyptian's conception of the *ka*, man's astral body. His curiosity about death and its customs feeds his insatiable desire for immortality.

Most of these ideas are fragmentary, some are inappropriate. Gironella is still reluctant to make an outspoken political judgment concerning the present regime. On being asked what lay before the government should Franco die, Gironella mildly answers, "I don't know what to tell you. I'm a humble man."[9] He refuses to discuss the current policy of continuism and avoids the question. Conversely, he is at his best when he discusses serious ideas pertaining to himself and his intellectual development. His strength as a writer is his sincerity in admitting to weakness.

The reports of his daily experiences in Egypt, Ceylon, and India provide few illuminations about Gironella the man. But Gironella's ability to describe and capture a particular setting in clearly written prose is his talent. His first impressions of Egypt may be usual to any tourist. Gironella evokes the realities vibrantly through his choice of just detail: "Quickly, I noted two common qualities: the filth—tattered clothing, disgustingly dirty hands and crusted dirt on bare feet and disease—eyes that looked

sick. Yes, we are in Egypt, country of endemic illnesses...."[10]
Putting into Port-Safagan, the "Almudena" waits a few days
before entering the Red Sea. Gironella's narration of his Egyptian
experiences is exciting and colorful. Once off the boat, he visits
the port and describes his impressions: "The sight of the mosque
in the center of town; the presence of ragged children with sick
eyes; the immobility of old men who fish by the pier; the absence
of women; the severe nature of the food. I wonder what the
inhabitants of Safagan really eat?"[11] Gironella puts many rhetorical questions and answers them in conversation with Georges
Imbert, in an effort to describe Arab life. He discusses the Arab
legacy as "... fatalism and women dressed in black,"[12] and proceeds to Mohammed, Islam, the Koran as compared to the
Bible. In Port-Safagan, he notes a total disregard and ignorance
of modern science, the sad lot of the female, eternally obedient,
the need for hygienic legislation for the entire community.

Again, contrasting East and West, Gironella reaffirms his belief
in the three influences at the foundation of Western civilization
—Hellenism, Rome, and Christianity. He condemns the West for
its dedication to materialism, its pleasures, Communism, the
atomic bomb, for all its short-sightedness. By including many
unimportant events, Gironella constrains his journal to report a
step-by-step account of his daily movements. Only when he picks
up the thread does the narrative live. The desert, at first rocky
and mountainous, then dominated by sand dunes interspersed
by oases, exalts Gironella. Children running barefoot over burning sands, the Bedouins on camels, Coca-Cola signs in the middle
of the desert, the stench, and the Oriental flies, are all part of
this new world. "For the first time, I made contact with the
oftentimes described African and Oriental stench. Stench of
bodies sweating, of animal excrement. Stench of slaughterhouses
filled with flies. The stench that incrusts itself in the nose and in
the brain like an unexpected blasphemy."[13]

En route by train from Kena to Luxor, Gironella is stimulated
to reflect—the immobility of Egyptian art, the excesses of Western conformity, leisure, alcohol, comfort, its dictatorships and
their repercussions. From Luxor to Thebes he is stirred by the
sight of the Nile and enthralled at the Valley of Kings: "The
modern tourist world is so alive that it *is* a reality so complete
in itself. Just as it concentrates its energies where there is much

activity, Cologne, Nice, Johannesburg, it does the same thing even where there are just stones. . . . We contemplated the spectacle in silence. The rockiness of the countryside immobilized our thoughts. . . . Discovering the amphitheatre with its own pyramid, the tourists were well satisfied since the pyramid alone signified the greatness of Egyptian civilization."[14] Gironella imagines the burial ceremonies, slaves at building the pyramids. His visit to the tombs of Tut Ankh-Amen and his realization that the dust he treads is the dust of those thousands of years dead arouse him. The artistry, creativity, and architectural imagination of the Egyptians impress him. Gironella tells of his experiences in tombs in detail—murals, the false tombs, graves, and rites of burial. The presence of Coca-Cola machines beside the tombs, so aesthetically upsetting, proves a necessity in the intense heat. Many of his Egyptian descriptions are excellent. "Luxor, Karnak . . . Signs indicating dates at the edge of the temples. Sphinxes with heads of rams, symbols of virility. The Sacred Lake where boats helped to furrow the land as cited in the liturgy in bygone days. Stones, stones, the remains of a race of giants."[15] "The colors of the rocks shot through by the sun—tiles of the tombs . . . and the white umbrella of our guide who accompanies us."[16] When Gironella makes an attempt to summarize the value of his experience, his immediacy and spontaneity fail.

Before leaving the port, he visits its bazaar, is besieged by a group of children begging for chocolates, and is depressed. Visits to a mosque, an Arab barber, a Franciscan school, and a souvenir stand are equally depressing although Gironella finds peace in the Franciscan chapel and weeps in solitude. He welcomes the sight of the freighter and embarcation for Asia and the East.

As the "Almudena" makes for Aden, meditation was an absolute necessity for Gironella. He speculates, envisaging the sea as a huge cemetery where fish like worms eat away the drowned bodies of men. A rainbow is the "eyebrow of God." With nothing to do, he constantly redefines the meaning of natural phenomena. Night is "a black abyss,"[17] and sea spray, "fertile and light, what is born and dies . . . the joyfulness of the sea, its venial sin, the consoling cry in the night of dark sea."[18] The "Almudena's" stop in Aden is short—a minor revolution forces the ship to leave early. The tedium of the sea is unbroken once more until they reach Ceylon.

Gironella has time to explore several ideas as they cross the Indian Ocean. As he examines his technique of observation, he notes, "Attentive and minute observation makes me discover laws that haste commonly hides from me. Laws of coherence, of harmony, and of compensation. Basically, all things always lead to a single objective, to a concrete terminus in time."[19] He elaborates on his conception of death—"joint operations of the body that convert us into live beings who keep on preparing for their death."[20]

In preparation for Ceylon, Gironella reads a biography of Ghandi and tourist manuals. The sea and his transistor radio occupy his thoughts until the "Almudena" comes to port. Since its cargo of phosphate is for tea plantations in the provinces, the ship's destination is altered from Colombo, the capital, to Trincomalee. It is a disappointment, but Gironella accepts it and rationalizes: "Ah! If we could visit the forests full of panthers, elephants, serpents. . . ."[21] While waiting to dock, Gironella subjects *Persons, Ideas and Seas* to criticism. His wife reads *Persons* in its entirety and feels it is essentially a simple diary, nothing more. She also criticizes its shallowness and imprecision: "It's turning out to be a dogmatic work."[22] The diary does reflect Gironella's skill in objective description but since his specific material is rarely integrated into a larger context, the result is unimportant. The Ceylon chapter continues the same pattern established for Egypt—a report of experience with little selectivity or profundity.

His descriptions of Ceylon, of Hindus and sacred cows, his short review of Ceylon's history and attempts to trace philological meanings of Indian words add little substance. So, too, Gironella's reactions to new foods and people lack any individual flavor. He attempts too much and the result has no significance. This fault is common to Egyptian, Ceylonese, and Indian chapters in style and content. With the exception of a few excellent descriptions, these chapters consist of a smattering of superficialities.

Gironella's visit to a Hindu temple is the first attempt at the meaning of religion. He meets a leper, films water buffalo, discovers a rain forest. The freighter is ordered to proceed to Pakistan rather than to India. Gironella must either continue with the ship or fly to India. He shortens his stay in Ceylon, summarizing major impressions of his journey: "Goodbye to

adventure on the freighter, to the Mediterranean and its beacons
in the night, to the Red Sea where the Hebrews travelled, to
Safagan where children threw stones at us, to Aden and its
marvelous toys, to the East, sultry, humid, a satellite splitting in
space, to Trincomalee with its Hindu temples and lepers. . . ."[23]
In this quotation Gironella evaluates himself. He has achieved
little but Gironella cannot risk interruption in continuity if he is
to achieve anything. In Colombo and before his departure by air
to Bombay, he describes the architectural plan of the capital and
its chalk-white façades shining in filth and misery. At a celebration of his departure with the "Almudena's" crew, the Gironellas
feel solitary and isolated. "I am sorry we separated. But I know
that such is life."[24]

The Indian phase is repetitious but since India in 1963 is appre-
hensive of a threat of invasion by Communist China, Gironella
is aroused in his air-conditioned hotel in Bombay to experience
through his senses the sights, sounds, tastes of India "with fresh
perspective."[25] Circling Bombay by taxi, he notes the tremendous
English influence, the cotton spinning mills, the castes, the city's
hedonist spirit, and the chaos of the slums.

Almost submerged by the teeming crowds of Bombay's streets,
the Taj Mahal Hotel reassures him in its organization, modernity,
and air conditioning. The overwhelming heat forces him to see
Bombay in long, early evening walks from the hotel. His descriptions include an account of the principal castes, the relation of
each to Brahma, and a visit to a crematorium. Gironella never
forgets his interest in death in any form.

At Gironella's request, an Indian architect analyzes the East:
"In India, man is peaceful and conscious that life is nothing more
than to be lived."[26] Gironella denies any attachment to machines,
watches, whistles, or Western inventions. His own life is hardest
to endure, of course, whatever external aid he may enjoy.

Gironella admits he cannot identify with the country or its
customs and that he is alienated by India. Padre Molinet, a Spanish Jesuit priest, Catalan, and originally from Gerona, strengthens
Gironella to endure his "Spanishness" and solitude. The Jesuit's
chief commentary on seeing the author in Bombay is indicative
of Spain's new interest in things foreign: "It's good that Spaniards
travel. You've got to get out of your shell, eh?"[27] Gironella feels
compelled to ask a fundamental question about faith but leaves

it unanswered: "Where could I find 'absolute' faith, the kind of faith that has illuminated you?"[28]

On a later visit to the University of St. Francis Xavier, Gironella is joyful because most Spanish missionaries in Bombay are Catalan and Catalan priests are among the most erudite. Their fervor and dedication make them lose sight of problems of their mother country—Spain. His admiration for these missionaries is sincere but possibly tinged with the envy of a youthful dream unfulfilled. His conversations with them about Spain, however, irritate him since these missionaries abroad maintain a gentle, sentimental view of their nation.

After an Indian cinema, newsreels on Benares, the holy city of the Hindus, and conversations on the differences between religious life of Christians and that enjoined by Hindu codes, Gironella writes on Indian humanity and his own need for faith: "Man is so weak, he finds himself so helpless that he demands once and again tangible representations of Omnipotence, ... an omnipotent force that created the universe and man in his own image. Thus, his adoration of the sun, the wind, the volcanoes is explained. In the same way, the millions of divinities created by the Hindi may be explained. Man needs miracles and if the miracle doesn't occur, he invents one."[29] Gironella also discovers an Indian principle essential to his own existence—the love of life, in fact, this journey and *Persons* derives from his own love and appreciation for life.

Gironella shows some interest in the idea that many Indians are susceptible to Christianity, and conversion of an influential person is a goal of the Spanish Catholic Missionaries to India.

Gironella believes he has overcome his narcissism, his necessity to have satisfaction through himself, the two detrimental concepts of the Western world. He believes in his search for truth and feels his journey to the Orient helped him resolve personal doubts and difficulties. Above all, he reestablishes his spiritual freedom: "I refuse to use any points of reference. I rebel against any limitations."[30] He sums up his impressions of India just before his return to Barcelona via Rome. "Goodbye to the Taj Mahal Hotel, to the man frightened by doves, to the maids who polished floors with rags attached to their feet, to the poetess who wrote verses in Bengali, to the large windows of the parlor where the Mohammedans celebrated the signing of important contracts, where ex-maharajas sat looking at diamonds on their fingers, where the Cuban newlyweds talked of Fidel Castro. . . . [31]

As a consequence of his trip, Gironella decides to practice yoga, rationalizing, "many people are convinced by its dogmas because no one knows anything about them."[32] His Indian experience, hopefully, will lead him to a new world of spiritual growth in truth and reality.

In Barcelona once more, Gironella and his wife experience a closer spiritual union that strengthens their marriage. Nevertheless, *Persons, Ideas and Seas*, in itself, is an index to Gironella's perceptions. It is the work of a popular artist whose naïve egocentrism sometimes mars objectively realistic portrayals of considerable merit. However, the journal does afford an opportunity for vivid personal revelations.

II *Gironella in Japan*

His next travel book, *El Japón y su duende* (*Japan and Her Ghosts*), answers to his desire to return to the Orient and deals with Gironella in Japan. He seeks to escape from the monotony of Europe to the vitality of Asia, searching for such a dynamic experience as will enlarge the Spaniard's and Spain's international horizons. Coincidentally, Narciso Yepes, an old friend and well-known guitarist, invited Gironella to accompany him to Japan on a concert tour. In April, 1963, both men left Barcelona for Tokyo.

One fundamental difference between *Persons, Ideas and Seas* and *Japan and Her Ghosts* is the seriousness of *Japan*. It is no collection of random notes but a highly organized and scholarly attempt to portray contemporary and traditional Japan. Its Table of Contents and Bibliography, well organized and impressive, show research and reflection. The volume has two parts—a description of Japan and "Psychological Anecdotes" by other hands, whose purpose is to penetrate into Japanese tradition more deeply than is possible for Gironella.

The introduction to *Japan and Her Ghosts*, describing preparations for the journey, is six pages in length. A series of subject headings in each chapter precedes each paragraph as preparation for the text. He is most successful as an observer and writer as he presents his original view of life among the Japanese.

His first impressions of Tokyo, its streets and architecture, seem to grope for orientation. As usual, in his explorations of Tokyo, he is preoccupied by death and insanity: "Yes, wherever I go, the first thing I do is to investigate how they live and where, the dead as well as the insane."[33] These are major in his excursions throughout Japan. These aside, *Japan* is objective and concrete as analysis of Japanese life rather than a subjective exposition of Gironella himself. He sees Japan intellectually, visiting huge factories to understand Japanese character, taking periodic walks through Tokyo streets to feel the presence of their multitudes, attending lectures for explanations of religious and philosophical implications of Bushido. He is impersonal and his conclusions seem authentic and authoritative.

His chapter about the Japanese woman, her recent emancipation, her traditional obedience to male authority, the effect of World War II upon her status, the training of the Geisha—all are related in Gironella's new scholarly, objective style. Its emphasis on documentation and objectivity makes *Japan and Her Ghosts* read as an historical rather than a personal view. Whereas *Persons, Ideas and Seas* reports a multitude of experiences extremely personally and unselectively, *Japan* is disciplined and detached. Gironella's chief problem in *Japan* is to channel the vitality of his personality. Such descriptions as those of a traditional dance in vivid detail and of a visit to a geisha establishment with Narciso Yepes are colorful. Dialogue aids in establishing immediacy and spontaneity. There is, however, little use of dialogue in *Japan*, and Gironella cites authorities on Japan and their quotations rather than descriptions of his own composition.

When the occasion requires, Gironella describes his visit to the home of Nakura Shumiza, famous artist in ceramics. Their discussion involves the predictable subject of East and West. The Shumiza family does help corroborate preconceptions of the author—the tense Japanese love of nature, trees, and small animals. The dinner and entertainment at the Shumiza home are quite traditional but the most interesting discussion is that between Gironella and Taiko, a university student.

Gironella is quick to perceive the youth's depression because of his obvious alienation from tradition. He soothes him, listening as Taiko, a product of World War II, reveals biographical details and where he lost his family. He was depressed and contemplating suicide. Gironella tries to console him, suggests that he become Christian and includes Taiko's atypical biography as evidence of the state of mind often to be found beneath the surface of Japanese youth. It is also evidence of the conflict of modern and traditional Japan.

Gironella's visit to the island of Oshima, his ascent of Mt. Mihara-Yama, his delight in natural beauty and the delicacy of Japanese art, are excellent. Certain comments on experiences at Hiroshima lead Gironella to a detached historical discussion of the Japanese attack on Pearl Harbor and the United States' offensive. His conclusion is that the grounds for conflict still continue, chiefly because Japan, despite her highly industrialized economy, prefers her Asian orientation to American influences. Gironella considers it inevitable that Japan will become the ally of Red China. His sober tone exhibits the historian and has a ring of uncomfortable but possible truth.

In lighter vein, Gironella relates his experiences in Nagasaki, his visit to the Atomic Bomb Garden and the hospitals for patients suffering the effects of radiation. He speculates whether the atomic bomb promoted conversions from Shintoism to Christianity. From this he embarks on a long discussion of Christianity in Japan and also notes the tendency of modern Japanese to repudiate Christianity as they do all religious ties for an agnosticism leaving room only for the cinema, sports, and sex.

In Hiroshima, Gironella compiles material on the first American atomic attack from eyewitness accounts. A brief history of the explosion, its devastation, its psychological and medical repercussions, lead to many pages on the new ultramodern Hiroshima. He visits a museum to the Hiroshima victims, Peace Park, and a hospital for the maimed. In a local night club, young people do the twist. Their capacity to enjoy themselves continues.

The only pastoral episode in *Japan and Her Ghosts* is Gironella's visit to Miyajima. In it he describes the land and its surrounding sea simply and with a real appreciation of the beauty. Nara and Nikko, their shrines and mausoleums, compare with the description of his Egyptian visit to the Valley of Kings. He no longer relies on the opinions of guide books but Gironella sees and tells in vivid and richly descriptive passages what he himself knows. His summary impression of Japan is poetic and moving: "The Orient puzzled me. On one hand, I couldn't avoid it. I felt it was alien and hostile. On the other hand, it fascinated me in an irresistible manner. It occurred to me that I was like a traveller who penetrated into the forest, in ecstasy because of the visual beauty of the trees. I realized that thousands of beings from an unknown world hid from my eyes."[34]

Gironella is like most foreigners and he cannot hope to comprehend fully Japan and its dynamic and constantly changing culture. He learns more from his interpreter Mikedo and Taiko, the student, than from his visits. "Japan had been an education, a riddle, a game of prestidigitation. It had brought me to a magical point, almost to a state of hypnotism."[35]

In his "Anecdotario psicológico" ("Psychological Anecdotes"), Gironella selected a series of texts from a wide bibliographical listing including authors such as Blasco Ibáñez and Lin Yutang to amplify his impressions of themes discussed in *Japan*. Perhaps characteristically, there is no identification of author or of source for his chosen quotations.

III   *Gironella's Travel Books Compared*

Although *Japan and Her Ghosts* appears more scholarly and contains much information about the Japanese, it usually lacks the vitality of the personal approach and dialogues of *Persons, Ideas and Seas*. Neither work is completely unified. Still, Gironella's *Japan and Her Ghosts* blends perspicacity of observation with greater selectivity in experience. Excision of trivia, freedom from bondage to chronology, and selectivity in the choice of thoughts and impressions, all contribute to a new standard of objectivity and artistic creation.

Gironella has gained immeasurably in his analysis and evaluation of political factors. The emergence of this quality and its dominance over these travel books promises new strength to his continuing career. *Persons, Ideas and Seas* initiated his interest and *Japan and Her Ghosts* sustained this interest with more serious historical foundations. The latter shows that a new transitional Gironella is becoming not only an essayist, but social critic and historian as well. His next work may have significance beyond Spain.

CHAPTER 10

Essayist, Social Critic, Historian

JOSÉ María Gironella's last two books, *Persons, Ideas and Seas* and *Japan and Her Ghost*, were a success in Spain because of their timely subject matter and colloquial style. The author, however, displayed greater seriousness of purpose and integrity in a group of six essays published in 1961. Some of these essays were virtually unnoticed, eclipsed by Gironella's fiction. Two of these contained preliminary ideas expanded into larger works which demonstrated more crystallization in style, thought, and content than that of either *Persons* or *Japan*. These two essays, "Viaje en torno a la revolución cubana" ("Journey into the Cuban Revolution") and "Viaje en torno a la revolución china" ("Journey into the Chinese Revolution"),[1] are the microcosm for Gironella's serious interpretations of politics and history although two others, "Rumbo a América" ("Heading for America") and "Las tres Europas" ("Three Different Europes"), are a mixture of personal and political thoughts.

A. *Impressions of America*

"Heading for America" presents in detail Gironella's thoughts before and during his trip to America. Before arriving in the United States, he planned his visit. "I have several projects in the United States: to travel through them, visit an atomic center and a modern neurological clinic, to see people of every race walking in the streets, to compare the country with the image we Spaniards have of it through literature and the movies, to interview Werner Von Braun and President Kennedy."[2] This formidable list of projects represents an ideal of significant activities and Gironella's outlook is generally hopeful and optimistic. He has many preconceptions concerning American life: "The empire of the dollar? Children growing up too fast? Bubble gum, sky-

scrapers, gasoline pumps, detestable English?"[3] Before boarding
the freighter "Covadonga" in Bilbao, Gironella declares his position as a writer: "I am not a philosopher, or a political observer
or even a newspaper correspondent. I'm a man who seeks to
investigate the reasons for things, to look for a synthesis."[4]

Much as for his Far Eastern journeys, Gironella describes
Bilbao, Lisbon, Cadiz, New York, Havana, and Vera Cruz. Although he reveals little about the European cities because he
spends relatively little time in them, he chooses to discuss the
emigration problem of Galicia, his lively fascination with Galician
dialects, and his unbearable sadness. Minor episodes aboard ship
occupy his thoughts from Cadiz until the "Covadonga" docks in
New York harbor. He fights boredom with meditation, seasick-
ness with medication. Arriving in New York City, Gironella
learns that the three public figures he cared to visit are preoccupied with health or political problems and unavailable for interviews. With a promise he might meet Adlai Stevenson at a later
date, he visits the Empire State Building, St. Patrick's Cathedral,
and the United Nations Building. His impressions of the city are
typical: "They had strange eyes, cheekbones, and chins. Inbreed-
ing among races resulted in, at times, very beautiful offspring. At
other times, the worst horrors. . . . Never had I seen so many
things prohibited in New York—no parking, smoking, pull don't
push, no turns, etc. . . ."[5] Although he is usually serious, Gironella's comment after reading a sign on a confessional booth in
St. Patrick's is amusing: "A multi-lingual confessor, perhaps because people can sin in all languages."[6] After a rapid survey of
Manhattan, he concludes pessimistically that New York is a city
". . . of turbulence, a fabulous sepulchre for the living."[7]

Unable to interview Adlai Stevenson at the United Nations,[8]
his visit there reveals Gironella's response to its architecture and
function. He dislikes its functional design and frigidity, the superficiality of the guides, modernity in its chapel which destroys
inspirational values.

Gironella reasserts that America is a world power but that
Americans are group-directed, socialized propagators of freedom.
They are materialistically minded, unified in statehood but,
otherwise, individually oriented. America's strength is her vigor
and power to unite in collective action and that she sacrifices
individual to group will. Gironella condemns prejudice against

Negroes since he says it does not exist in European nations. If America effectively controls half of the world, he offers little political commentary but suggests Europeans are superior. Americans are a group of parvenus, culturally debased, and with a short-lived role of political dominance which will revert to Europe.

This essay lacks profundity of observation and penetration of thought and what power it has comes from Gironella's logical analysis. After six weeks in New York City, unable to communicate in English, and meeting relatively few Americans and their families, Gironella's view of America was inaccurate. His subsequent travel books increasingly contain illuminating reports of personal interviews, visits to homes of friends and nationals, and accounts of tours other than those to principal points of interest. Thus he gives a more accurate picture of each particular locale. Again, Gironella proves to be a serious and yet timid observer. He is overwhelmed by the impact of New York so that his descriptions of the city smack of awe, even of humility. These early essays lack indulgent witticisms and his personal comments are more sober, honest, and generally given to naïveté.

B. *A Sociological View of Europe*

"Las tres Europas" ("Three Different Europes") is Gironella's modest attempt at a sociological problem by utilizing his senses and critical spirit to describe the diversity of the European community. "I do not pretend to have made any discoveries and I've resisted the temptations of writing from shallow impressions on this matter; rather, I am proceeding with my thoughts based only upon my intuition."[9]

Europe falls into three geographical zones—a northern, southern, and central sphere. Through conversations with representatives from each geographical area, considering language and vocabulary the most revealing factor in personality, he examines the southern temperament first. His conclusions echo those already famous of Salvador de Madariaga. Gironella establishes his ability to analyze psychological data capably and to perform penetrating research. Some comments on Spain are noteworthy.

Gironella cannot understand the Spaniard's resistance to abstract concepts and concludes this is the reason for the scarcity of Spanish philosophers. Southern Europeans are not vital be-

cause of centuries of poverty, climatic conditions inducing laziness, and a failure of Catholicism to aid in a restoration of
self-confidence. Gironella accuses the southerner of being subservient, inferior, and of hiding himself behind the figure of
Christ.

His analyses of central and northern Europeans lead Gironella
to conclude that Europe represents a perfect and harmonious
unity of men, ideas, and values. He advocates Pan-Europeanism
and a united world community.

"Three Different Europes" indirectly restates Ortega y Gasset's
desire for European solutions to solve Spain's political, economic,
and social problems. Gironella is one of the few contemporary
novelists aware of the enormous possibilities of expansion for
Spain if she enters the European Common Market. Since 1961,
Gironella developed an intense interest in politics and problems
of other nations. He seeks to foster among Spaniards a cosmopolitanism and international understanding. His analysis of
communism in Cuba and China derives from his interest in political and social problems beyond Spain. His vital interest in social
revolutions of all kinds combines with his passion for history and
social problems to produce his explanation of the appeal of Communist ideology. Two lengthy essays present his personal view of
the significance of communism in China and Cuba. He longs for
political involvement but has no opportunity under the present
régime.

C. Cuba and the Revolution

"Viaje en torno a la revolución cubana" ("Journey into the
Cuban Revolution") narrates Gironella's experiences on a visit
to Cuba in 1960. His essay on China, however, is the result of
research in Spain after his return from Japan in 1962. The essays
show great stylistic differences chiefly because of the fluctuations
of the writer's methods of reporting. "Journey" was first published
in 1961 as a personal memoir of his observations of the Castro
régime then just coming to power. Its five chapters trace Gironella's journey from New York to Havana and his return to Spain.
The first two chapters are retrospective and an historical introduction to the Cuban crisis. They show considerable cohesion
in style and thought.

The first chapter discusses important events in Cuba's history, such as the rise of the dictatorship of Fulgencio Batista and Cuba's relationship with the United States. The very important first paragraph (cut from the English translation) presents Gironella's condemnation of President Kennedy for his vacillation during the "missile crisis" which subjected Cuba to the probability of becoming a Russian satellite. Gironella maintains that the Movement of July 26 was a consequence of corruption and Batista's régime in particular. Gironella considers Cuba the trouble spot of the Western Hemisphere because of the constant North-American exploitation of her industry and resources, and the United States' continued recognition of the corrupt Batista régime. Consequently, the slow appeal and take-over of communism was caused directly by the abuses of capitalism. Although Fidel Castro originally expressed intentions of agrarian reform, the author believes that he did nothing useful except to create a renaissance of a Mafia type and that he was handing Cuba over to a set of Russian masters.

Emphasizing the imperialist role of the United States since 1898 as economic oppression, Gironella demonstrates how Communist ideology superseded that of capitalism, how Fidel Castro, the combination intellectual-economist-historian-lawyer, becomes the symbol for a new Cuba, and how Cubans were betrayed by the "olive-green" revolution.

The second chapter gives an incisive portrait of Castro, whom Gironella sees as enigmatic, volatile, and self-contradictory. His Catholic background and upbringing, his dedication to the political ideas of Cuba's leading patriot, José Martí, his agitation for reform are the principal facets of his personality. They result finally in his new role of Communist demagogue. Gironella describes Castro as an erratic whose exceptional oratorical gifts and thorough legal background destine him to be Cuba's new leader against overwhelming odds. He can even be compared to Salvatore Giuliano, Sicily's famed "Robin Hood" hero-bandit. Castro's gradual commitment to communism, under the guidance of his brother Raúl and the Argentine Che Guevara, after his victory in a guerrilla war is emphasized. Employing the three weapons of all dictatorships, repression, public spectacles, and lies, Castro is condemned by Gironella as an exponent of Hitlerism. The wave of mass demonstrations, propaganda, nationalization of industries, anti-Catholic purges, pave the way for the

Kremlin's easy intervention in Cuba. Gironella considers Castro comparable to Hitler or to Lenin.

Gironella's portrait of Castro is a carefully drawn indictment of a man who betrayed his nation and reflects Gironella's passion as a champion of freedom appealing to democracy-loving citizens everywhere to see that the Cuban example should never be repeated.

The final three chapters of the Cuban essay contain Gironella's personal impressions of his trip aboard the vessel "Guadalupe" written in the familiar style of *Persons, Ideas and Seas.* His observations, however, prove to be exciting because of the intense drama inherent in the Cuban political situation. As a result of Castro's seizure of power, Gironella becomes interested in the comments of Cuban exiles returning home with new illusions, patriotic fervor, fanaticism, and anti-American. A single interview with a recruiter for *Citizens of the New Cuba* reveals Gironella's informant to be pro-Communist, anti-Semitic, and a puppet product of Kremlin propaganda. The third chapter also establishes Gironella's personal opposition to Communism, his mistrust of Russian politics, and his fear of Castro's Cuba.

The fourth chapter narrates his impressions of teeming Havana with government censorship offset by spectacular Communist propaganda parades. In Havana the "Guadalupe" is greeted with cries of "¡Cuba sí, yanquis no!". In one day ashore, he notes the great number of militia, guns, Russian products, Russian-published revolutionary periodicals, even a film showing of Russian Cinerama. He notes the patriotic fervor of the new militiamen, the absence of propaganda concerning agrarian reform or increased medical services. Castro's literacy campaign alone remains a publicized issue of the revolution.

He passes a funeral service for one of the many Cubans killed in battle and he is aware of the irreligious manner in which the burial is conducted. Later in the day, his attendance at a monster rally by Castro's Rebel Youth and Young Pioneers recalls visions of Hitler's *Bund* rallies during the 1930's. After spending an exhausting day in Havana, he returns to the "Guadalupe" to watch a Havana television broadcast of an anti-Franco rally in which Eugene Lister, the infamous exiled Spanish Communist, preaches his philosophy to Cubans and paves the way for Cuban acceptance of the Soviet Union's "great sacrifice" to help Cuba gain peace.

The final chapter of Gironella's Cuban adventures is the most moving. Before the "Guadalupe" sails back to Spain, it takes many Cuban refugees on board. The author's portrayal of a ninety-six-year-old Catholic Mother Superior kissing the ground before coming aboard the "Guadalupe" and declaring that she will return to Cuba is most indicative of the tone of this chapter. He discusses the clerics' expulsion from Cuba, presents the plight of the political refugee in such graphic terms to recapture dramatically real events that have the evocative power of good fiction. Once on the open Atlantic, Gironella talks to these exiles, seeking information on the nature and extent of Catholic persecution in Cuba, and elicits from them the reasons for their expulsion. The revolution was "unexpected" and religious persecution had the same unpredictability. These clergy believe Castro intends to make Cuba an agency to disseminate communism in the Western Hemisphere. Before their arrival in Galicia, they finally calmed down although deep resentment for the Castro régime showed in their conversations. Gironella believes that political and economic pressure of the European community can liberate Cuba from its oppressors. The European continent, he feels, is the only savior since other national powers are politically concerned elsewhere. "Russia and the United States can reach for the moon, and China for the highest population. But Europe should stay close to the Earth. To stay close to the Earth more than ever because Europeans know how to deal with their problems. They have made the Earth beautiful and prosperous."[10] Gironella's earlier proclamation for Pan-Europeanism is his outstanding contribution to political thought and concerted European intervention is a possible solution for Cuba.

Contrary to other Spanish writers visiting Cuba during this time of crisis, Gironella had no sense of identification with a former colony but predicts the downfall of Cuban communism because the spirit of a once-free nation cannot die. Gironella is concerned not only with Cuba's freedom, but with Catholicism. In a prologue to the English translation of his essay, John F. Byrne explains his concern: "Gironella's preoccupation with communism as a socio-historical phenomenon is due to the violent eruption it has caused in contemporary history; his deeper preoccupation is related to the fact that its enormous vigor and apostolic zeal of its disciples have stolen the role of moral and

social pacesetter which once corresponded to Christianity."[11]
Since Cuba shared Spanish-Catholic tradition for many centuries,
the point is of interest.

D. *Gironella on China*

China's own religious, ethical, and cultural background insure
that adherence to Communist ideology derives from a totally
different source. In his essay "Viaje en torno a la revolución
china" ("Journey into the Chinese Revolution"),[12] Gironella understands the effectiveness of Communist ideology, and China
is its most extensive stage setting. Nevertheless, he doubts its
complete success because of Mao Tse-tung's independent attitude
to Russian policy as compared to Fidel Castro's total dependence.
In three chapters which John Byrne says are characteristic of
the author's "austere grey prose, shot through with rare unexpected shafts of brilliant sunlight,"[13] Gironella discusses China's
historical evolution from Communist satellite to independence
from Russia. His final chapter is an analysis of communism
versus Christianity and includes Gironella's motivations for research into the political affairs of China and Cuba, two nations
at the geographic poles of communism.

By a series of rhetorical questions, Gironella sets forth a brief
history of China in his first chapter, ending in praise for Mao
Tse-tung, poet-political writer-agitator, China's dictator through
whom corruption and vice will end in industrialization and communism. Since Christianity is not a major issue for Mao Tse-tung,
an easy success for Communist doctrine is assured.

Chapter Two contains a biography of Mao. It traces his. career
through his early days with the Communist Party, his rise, his
rivalry with Chiang Kai-shek and the famous "Long March" of
1934, his formation of the first commune in Yenan (1935), and
leadership of the first Communist military dictatorship in China.
China changes from a democracy to socialism and finally emerges
after thirty years a Communist satellite. Chiang and a few thousand soldiers seek refuge in Formosa (Taiwan), today the
stronghold of Nationalist China.

Gironella's third chapter discusses Mao's success as a political
leader. He treats of Mao's programs of industrialization, nationalization, agrarian reform, his alliance with Russia and her technique of the Five Year Plan, repression, propaganda, and public

works. For Gironella, Chinese communism is overwhelming if only because of China's enormous physical scale. Catastrophes like floods have their epic proportions because they set back many years the advancement of the Communist régime. Within the party, Gironella describes "purifications" caused by the rise of communes and discusses the evolution of a new elite corps, *Kun-pa,* birth control, campaigns against illiteracy, reforestation and xenophobia; Gironella emphasizes the frightening significance of the fact that all lives are public property, a reigning principle of Chinese communism denying at once individuality and independence. He quotes from Chou En-lai's summary speech of Communist ideals: "The Christians trust in God. The Humanists trust in man's capacity. We Marxists trust in the products of nature and in the economical use one makes of them."[14] This is the essential theme of Mao's revolution.

The fourth and final chapter presents Gironella's case that communism be considered a fruit of the evils of capitalism. Unfortunately, in its protest, it became a dictatorship itself because of its insistence on the principle of the collective. He notes Mao's oppression of Christianity and his substitution of "dialectical materialism" for attainment of values he desires. Gironella here also contrasts communism and capitalism as diametrically opposed. He believes Christianity, based on love, operating in a society where evolution from the creative act of God results in moral good and ultimately achieves perfection to be superior to Communist ideology. Communism is founded on hatred. Its evolution and perpetuation are dependent on the class struggle. Moral goodness, to be Communist, derives from a breakdown of capitalism.

Gironella's implicit political comments are more important than his historical investigations. In this essay on China, Gironella analyzes the Communist threat and its preparation in a godless, unchristian world. His feeling for Christianity is intense and, indirectly, he presents his statement of his belief in God.

The essays on China and Cuba not only elevate the novelist to the status of political observer but to a position as a provocative, sympathetic analyst, sustained by personal conviction in the Christian ideal and the democracy of the Western world. Therefore, these essays, in comparison to his more popular travel books, are politically oriented and well narrated with portraits of distinct nations, and shed new perspective on Gironella's changing values.

Gironella's publishers thought that his essays, which appeared chronologically earlier than *Persons, Ideas and Seas* or *Japan and Her Ghosts* should be reissued. The increasing ideological importance of Communism also caused his publishers to reprint Gironella's essay on China in a new, updated and expanded version. The scarcity of such work in Spain is generally acknowledged. Its timeliness and his publishers' insistence that Gironella appear as political spokesman to prepare the public for him in this role when a third volume of his Civil War trilogy finally appeared combined for republication of *Journey into the Chinese Revolution.*

E. A Reappraisal of China

China, lágrima innumerable (*China, Countless Tears*) is a slightly expanded version of the aforementioned original essay with addition of sixty-four black-and-white photographs. A new prologue to this work tells that the idea for this work resulted from actual contact with Chinese exiles whom Gironella met in Ceylon and Japan and former Christian and Catholic missionaries now in Formosa. He did not record their observations but his interpretation of the Chinese problem rests on their accounts. The additions to the new text are minimal.

After closely examining the original essay in translation and in this new version, differences of some importance are apparent. In the first chapter, Gironella quotes Giovanni Papini in a prophesy concerning China. It is a biological necessity which impels the Chinese to dominate the lands about them and to expand their domains. Papini considers the displacement of the Chinese as a move to dominion and his prophesy envisages hard, cruel, Chinese rule after a few generations. "The 'yellow' danger will change inside of some generations into complete domination by the yellow race. Their dominion will neither be soft nor easy."[15] So, too, Gironella perceives the Chinese migration as a result of overpopulation since one out of every four of the world's inhabitants is Chinese. Papini's prophesy is fast becoming historical fact. Gironella also believes that Tibet, Korea, and Indochina are mere geographical extensions of this Chinese population expansion.

The title, *"China, Countless Tears,"* derives from his original text and Gironella's conviction that Mao Tse-tung and his triumph will *not* alter China's destiny as a "valley of tears." New subject headings for thematic divisions and a series of pedantic footnotes confuse rather than illuminate.

Textually, Chapter Three of the translation concentrates on Mao's role as the key to China. This new edition presents the career of Liu Chao-chi, "the man without a face," executor of Mao's policies. Liu also advocates China as a nuclear power, provides impetus for ethnic and anthropological studies, encourages technology, and elevates the new China to the status of an international but politically unrecognized power. Gironella defines the "holy trinity" of Red China—Mao in ideology, Liu in scientific technology, and Chou in political acumen.

Another new section discusses China's role as a nuclear power because of the efforts of Dr. Chien Sen-chiang (the best-known nuclear physicist in China), Mao's political and territorial expansion into Tibet and India, and Peking's political rupture with Moscow. He describes Mao's victory over the Dalai Lama and Tibet with a description of the bloody Chinese assault on Lhasa and the country's complete surrender. India's intimidation by Mao was a conscious attempt to disseminate Chinese Communist ideology over all Asia. Chinese missions to Central Africa, Viet Nam, and Cuba cause the rupture with Russia although ideology is probably the underlying cause. Gironella believes basic demographic differences between Russians and Chinese would have caused a political schism sooner or later. His view of China's ambition is characteristic of Gironella's political writings: "Russia will continue being, by measure of her strategic position, a 'travelling companion' but no longer 'an older sister.'"[16]

Many new ideas appear in this late edition—a possible entry of Red China into the United Nations, French recognition of China, political purges—all events which were not foreseeable in 1961. Also, in a new series of conclusions, Gironella acknowledges Mao's contributions to China. He predicts a new revolution since China condemns herself to political isolation after breaking relations with Moscow. He speculates about eventualities after Mao's death, but concludes China's destiny will be guided by God. A godless and Communist China is doomed and will disappear as Chinese dynasties have in the past. China awaits ". . . a new stage along its road of irremediable pain."[17]

A new Epilogue analyzes Nationalist China, the miracle of Formosa, as a gigantic military base, fortified by United States arms and monies. He points out that Formosa is ". . . a thorn driven into the heart of Communist China. . . ."[18] and that its existence causes Mao's régime to be on a continual alert. Although he does not foresee change in Chiang Kai-shek's régime, he feels a fusion of Nationalists and Communists will take place. It is historically inevitable.

China, Countless Tears is considerably improved, penetrating, provocative, and showing evidence of painstaking research. The inclusion of photographs are well integrated with the text and lend deeper insights to descriptions, sometimes making words unnecessary. Those of executions and those of obvious accomplishments of Communist and Nationalist China are good examples. For the first time, photographs appear in a publication of Gironella. His care in selection helps to elaborate realistic prose passages and shows Gironella's artistic restraint. *China* is the author's best political work to date.

CHAPTER 11

Autocritic and Literary Analyst

I *Essays on the Art of Writing*

THE period 1953-1961 was creative and fertile, for in it Gironella published a wide variety of essays, newspaper articles,
short stories, and novels. The essay sections of *Phantoms of My
Brain* and *We Are All Fugitives* establish Gironella as literary
analyst, self-critic, and possibly, as biographer.

In 1953, Gironella's brief article "Dificultad de los géneros
literarios" ("The Difficulty with Literary Genres") was published
in *Arriba*. In it he analyzes difficulties besetting a writer, and
warns the public not to confuse talent with tenacity. Although
the novel is probably the easiest genre to approach, Gironella
holds that, for it, "experienced" reality is not enough. The novel
must conform to an ideal, the artistic transposition of life, and
must incorporate universal truths. Composition to be effective
demands documentation, imagination, and sensitivity. These
points recapitulate Gironella's thought of *Novelist Before the
World* and his references are obviously autobiographical.

Gironella revived the nineteenth-century realistic-historical
novel, and his interest in it continues. His lecture, "¿Por qué el
mundo desconoce la novela española?" ("Why Is the World
Ignorant of the Spanish Novel?"), at the Ateneo of Madrid in
1954 elaborated upon his discovery, confirmed during his European travels (1948-1952), that the Spanish novel was a minor
influence in Western literature. *Don Quixote*, a few novels of
Blasco Ibáñez, and fugitive editions of Alarcón, Palacio Valdés,
Valle-Inclán, and Pío Baroja comprise the Spanish authors repre-
sented in European libraries.

Gironella explained in his lecture that isolated and poverty-
stricken Spain had no cultural prestige, and that, consequently,
foreign publishers preferred to issue translations from the Span-

ish. Individual Spaniards lacked interest in literature and in
business sense, so the Spanish novel even had limited national
distribution. Unamuno, García Lorca, Ortega y Gasset, and
Gregorio Marañón have a restricted foreign public. Although
films and radio give some hope for breaking the cultural isolation of Spain, these media are usually highly selective and by no
means are free from distortion. Spaniards, including Spanish
authors, are clannish abroad, and Gironella considers this to be
a mark of a deeply seated feeling of inferiority. Hence, with isolated exceptions in the performing arts—Victoria de los Angeles,
José Iturbi, María Casares and Andrés Segovia—Spanish novelists, like all Spaniards, are almost unknown internationally.

During the Civil War, for lack of talent and lack of imagination, the novel did not exist in Spain. Gironella criticizes the
Generation of 1898 for neglect of the novel. He believes Gómez
de la Serna, Valle-Inclán, and Azorín wasted their extraordinary
talents on unclassifiable genres. He cites the comments of Azorín
and Baroja which disclose reasons for the lack of recognition of
the Spanish novel. Baroja believes Spaniards lack "constructive
imagination"; Valle-Inclán and Azorín write as *escritores-artistas*,
and as impressionists incapable of capturing truly great objective
events for the novel.

Also, the Spanish novel is regional without universal themes or
transcension of Spain. Paradoxically, Spanish novelists lack confidence in themselves. Thematically, most Spanish novels deal
with extraordinary problems rather than with normal concerns
of daily living. This, with the recent tendency of modern Spanish
novelists to choose improbable scenes for locales, to avoid reality,
is a result of *chulería* (literary bravado). Excessive exaggeration
of love, patriotism, or nobility compensate for their lack of confidence. Spain's decline as a colonial power and the power of
Franco's censorship also deal decisive blows at creativity.

Regeneration must result from self-control, the only method
by which creation can shape a work subjective but impartial,
artistically pure, and prophetically valid. Gironella remains pessimistic for he anticipates these endemic weaknesses will under-
mine any premature renaissance. "Our generation continues to
adolesce because of a pathological lack of imagination and it
continues to investigate the method of writing novels; techniques of counterpoint, syncopated chapters, flashback, etc., in

order to distract the public's attention."[1] Government censorship is no adequate excuse for mediocrity. Talent should not fail because of restraint, or need an impetus to action. If writers of this generation can do little to overcome censorship, they are blameworthy if they remain ignorant, insular, or undisciplined. Of course, Gironella's cosmopolitanism, so recently developed, had remedied any such weaknesses in him if, indeed, they ever existed. In a final admonition, Spanish atavism is a crushing limitation to universal acceptance. It must be abandoned.

Gironella's evaluation of the strengths and weaknesses of the novel is frank and always subjective. "Gironella makes a logical examination of a single literary genre [the novel] which he himself cultivates and is undoubtedly well acquainted with. His inventory of its qualities and defects, which was widely disseminated in Spain, includes frank, well-measured and revealing judgments. . . . This frankness with which Gironella has overthrown the orthodox barricades of peninsular thought has made him a literary revisionist whose voice will be heard throughout the world."[2] This article revealed acute perception and well considered, if rather superficial judgments. His most successful work, *The Cypresses Believe in God*, achieved international renown because Gironella had the awareness, courage, and spirit to transcend the restrictive traditions of the Spanish novel.

His essay, "Confesiones de un escritor" ("Confessions of a Writer") promises more than it really achieves. Gironella admits to an insatiable desire, from his early youth, to write. His early novels indicated he had many obstacles to overcome and his educational background was poor. His preferred authors, Papini, Ibáñez, Lin Yu-tang, Tagore, share a certain superficiality and indicate in him an inability for evaluation. A talent of the first rank like Cervantes is beyond him, as he is always open to a variety of external, usually secondary, influences. "I have always been weak and susceptible to influences, subdued by societal pressures to a large measure, subject to the whims of fortune. Many times, I ask myself, for example, would I be writing if civil war had not broken out . . ."[3]

By twenty-five, Gironella began to write short stories, religious discourses, and verse. He wrote hundreds of verses dedicated to his mother and innumerable letters in the trenches during the Civil War, as well as short theatrical pieces. All of these have disappeared. This apprenticeship taught him that the novel was the best form to "... write something broad and meaningful, to create a character and make him live an entire life...."[4] Fearful of censorship, Gironella nevertheless persisted in writing novels.

Gironella enjoys the power of influencing the ideas of others. Aware of his responsibility, and seeking perfection, Gironella is cognizant of the difficulties before him in a writing career. His earliest novels he considers *novelas pasatiempos* or light reading. Publication of *The Cypresses Believe in God*, his first serious novel, led to the genre of the *novela-ensayo* or "fictionalized essay" for his travels. His "confessions" are far from complete for now he shows interest in Camus, Toynbee, Salgado, and Matute.[5] Yet, Edward J. Gramberg believes that Gironella is lacking in the autocritical spirit.[6]

II   *Biographical Essays*

Gironella has always been attracted by biography but never attempted it as a major form suitable for his talent. A fictional tribute to Giovanni Papini excepted, only two men have figured in essays with a vague resemblance to biography. These two are Julián Marías, a Spanish critic, and Gironella's personal friend, the guitar player, Narciso Yepes. Each approaches biography in terms of personality.

Gironella wrote of Narciso Yepes after a two-day visit to his home in Madrid. Yepes appears as well-rounded, cultivated, intelligent, and talented as Gironella states he intends to present him: "In this article, I would like to tell faithfully how a boy from a town in Murcia, born in rubble and dust, arrived at the top in a few years to be Narciso Yepes, the outstanding guitarist."[7] Yepes' childhood in Lorca, his early music studies in Valencia, and his determination to continue his musical career despite financial difficulties all figure in the creation of his character as do romantic yearnings inspired by the sound of his guitar. "... and his guitar became a spirit through which his listeners discovered unknown depths within themselves."[8] Dramatic monologues add verisimilitude to this warmly colored sketch. Gironella worships at Yepes' shrine but cannot formulate objective conclusions. If Yepes is temperamental, he is also disciplined. His whole career from music student in Paris, his development of his own personal technique, and his ideal to make the guitar accepted internationally as a concert instrument, show these qualities. Yepes, as a true international artist shares with Gironella the concept of a European community. Gironella is dazzled by Yepes' mental and physical vigor which makes Gironella's two days at the Yepes home unforgettable. Yepes' portrait is rounded with the artist as gentle, loving husband, and upright man of extreme and honorable simplicity. "His actual plans are simple: to go on studying and to travel, giving concerts."[9] This sketch of Narciso Yepes is an evaluation not only of his talent but of the man himself. It is a tribute of appreciation and of love.

"Julián Marías, filósofo y articulista" ("Julián Marías, Philosopher and Journalist") in *La Jirafa*, 1958, is primarily an evaluation of Marías as philosopher. Marías' *"Aquí y ahora"* (*"Here and Now"*) leads Gironella to place him as an unoriginal eclectic whose startling phrases and unnecessary complexity conceal a lack of creative thought. For Gironella, Marías exemplifies two outstanding qualities of the Spanish writer: i.e., dogmatism, with a power to enlighten. Marías is admirable in that he has transcended his classical training and in his apposite comments on contemporary Spanish society, Marías' aesthetic approach, his lively prose, his cosmopolitanism and his willingness to learn, make him for Gironella a modern man and, more important, a modern Spaniard worthy to represent his generation. "I believe that Julián Marías may constitute in our vast sea, an island of salubrity."[10]

III   *Miscellany*

Gironella's fondness for the manipulations of statistics and of figures led to curious results. "Estadísticas sobre hombres célebres" ("Statistics on Famous Men"), prepared with the aid of the World Almanac and unidentified Dictionaries of Biography, is an inventory of "greatness" from the fifteenth through the twentieth centuries. Gironella's discussion is limited to writers, musicians, and painters with several arbitrarily chosen categories as referents, all as subjectively chosen as unoriginal.

Thus, France has contributed most writers, musicians, and painters but Germany is the cradle of great musicians. His chosen examples are placed chronologically and by nationality. To correlate age and genius, he lists the deaths of talented artists by decades; viz., between the ages of twenty-two and thirty, thirty and forty, forty and fifty. Coincidences as to birth and death fascinate him for he believes correlations may exist between artistic renown and professional abilities as sons of lawyers, bankers, painters.

His categories are artificial, his statistics pointless without the aid of subjective meanings Gironella assigns to them. Gironella seems to believe all great artists are isolated and that the melancholy caused by this solitude comes from within them. Their great gifts are frustrated as they create. Each creative artist also must surmount a series of inevitable and nearly overwhelming obstacles. Somewhat autobiographically, Gironella considers the nature of creativity: ". . . to create is to look for synthesis, permanence, to join, to cast over the disparate a blend of colors."[11] This statistical analysis proves to Gironella the great among artists, musicians, and novelists create joy and love such as may fill a void of human loneliness. His concluding reference to death and cemeteries may indicate the elaboration of a vast joke that Gironella has erected for his own entertainment: "In reality, I have concocted a 'paper' necrology, a cemetery in which are buried a good portion of wise men and world-famous artists."[12]

Nevertheless, Gironella leaves this ambiguity open, as he so often does. His statistical researches, as he lists them, contain a projected *Galerías de oficios* (*Occupational Handbook*), an alphabetical compendium of occupations. In it, he expects to analyze the unique, the original, and such occupations as defy proper classification.[13] This too may be an elaborate excursion into nonsense. On the other hand, he may consider it as a valid exercise for creative intelligence.

IV   *Autocriticism*

"Así escribí *Un millón de muertos*" ("Thus I Wrote *One Million Dead*") is really self-criticism, particularly since it contains autobiographical clues to understanding Gironella. Gironella describes himself as an idealistic skeptic, interested in science. His current subject of interest which lends itself to his peculiar statistical method is a possible category of myopia characteristic of great thinkers.[14] This may be connected with Gironella's mastery of medical terminology and study of causes and results of diseases which he described years ago after his own illness.

Gironella asserts he considers neither critics nor their opinions except for a few he left unnamed.[15] His wife and "best critic" is an exception. Still, in reply to criticism, Gironella wrote of his early and unsuccessful novel *Where the Soil Was Shallow*: ". . . my vanity suffered from a hard blow and I had a strange reaction: I began to read with morbid eagerness as many biographies about great writers that fell into my hands, with the sincere intention of discovering their secrets."[16] Gironella avoids discussion of adverse criticism of his early works but does in "Thus I Wrote *One Million Dead*" discuss the genesis and execution of his Civil War trilogy. The essay contains autobiographical details such as the growth of his progressive awareness of the value of trial and error in his novels. This essay documents admirably Gironella's problems of authorship and in this is its real value.

Gironella as critic is stronger in setting forth autobiographical details than he is in any other aspect of the art of criticism. He is admirably specific when he treats of himself and these essays add measurably to an understanding of the workings of his personality. Any criticism of his revelations of himself is that his remarks are usually superficial rather than indicative of a deep understanding either of himself or of his art.

CHAPTER 12

Gironella's Portrait of Franco's Spain:
Ha estallado la paz
(The Peace Has Broken Out)

H*A estallado la paz (época de posguerra) (The Peace Has
Broken Out)* (postwar epoch) continues *The Cypresses
Believe in God (época de anteguerra)* (prewar epoch) and *One
Million Dead (época de la guerra)* (war epoch). Gironella's
long-term intent for this novel was a conclusion to a three-volume
series, but an intention which he now repudiates:

This book, however, is not going to close the cycle. That is to say,
the original work I conceived, focused on our "national drama," will
not be a trilogy as was previously announced. Taking into account
that its historical-political phase which began in 1939 has not yet
ended and many of its problems fundamentally still endure, I have
decided to dedicate to the postwar phase several volumes. It does
not seem valid, in any aspect to end my panoramic view [of Spain]
on any particular year: 1945, 1950, 1958. . . . Neither is it feasible to
embrace in a single volume such a long period. Thus, I decided to
fragment it and write a kind of *Episodios nacionales* that could end
the day on which the succession of our Chief of State might take
place.[1]

In this, Gironella follows in the tradition of Pérez Galdós' *Episodios nacionales (National Episodes)*, but *The Peace Has Broken
Out* is the weakest novel of the original trilogy.

I *Content and Critical Analysis*

In this sequel, Gironella returns to the Alvears between 1939
and 1941 with two themes of importance—Spain's reconstruction
under Franco's nationalism, and romantic love. His fresco of
postwar Spain becomes a praise of Franco's nationalist reforms
seen in reference to Catalonia. Peaceful political rallies, fairs,

religious holidays, are colorfully narrated to emphasize the vital energy of Catalans in peacetime reconstruction. Gironella's knowledge of war and social revolution gained from his studies of China and Cuba is put to good use here in his descriptions of progressive reforms by the Nationalists. Gironella invokes a reunified Spain and the strong, fanatic spirit engendered under Franco:

The feeling of pride was strong, intense. Heroic deeds could be compared to those of Columbus, the Reconquest and victories against the Turks. With the result that all of Spain's provinces would be invited to present a commemorative gift to Franco, a replica of El Cid's famous sword. Then people would turn their energies to reconstruction. . . . The original idea of the Nationalist Revolt spearheaded by Franco was to incorporate into the hierarchy of government the ideas of race, country, nation and the spirit of God. In merging these ideas and by just acknowledging them so that they serve a Spain ruled by its Caudillo is, in itself, a religious act.[2]

Peace brings with it both desire and occasion for reform. Since Gironella's leitmotifs are freedom through ordered change and freedom through love, resentment against Franco is consistently minimized. Citing Papini, Gironella sets the tone for the novel: "In order to approach liberty, happiness, it's not enough to change the systems of government; one must change the spirits and hearts of men, of those who govern and are governed, of the rulers and their subjects, of those who command and those who must obey."[3] Gironella's chief concern is fictional rather than political, since Franco's solutions, which he accepts, leave the field free for development of individual patterns. War has ended and the Alvears are reunited. The family as a unit reappears. After the death of César, Matías and Carmen have matured through their suffering. (At one point, Carmen undergoes a hysterectomy.) Ignacio completes his law studies and finally receives his degree at the University of Barcelona. Pilar leads the Woman's Section for the Falange of Gerona. In her tense patriotism and love for Mateo Santos, also strongly Falangist, the problems of youth, especially love, receive a contemporary and political frame of reference. The spectre of death, so conspicuous in *One Million Dead*, disappears before the new vitality of Spain's reconstruction. Death is only mentioned in connection with a possibility of César's beatification. Three characters—

Ignacio, Pilar and their cousin Paz Alvear—and their personal decisions make up the essential intrigue of this novel. *The Peace Has Broken Out* is emphatically a novel of decisions as it is also one of postwar problems. New characters, new problems, give Gironella his widening canvas.

Ignacio Alvear is stronger for his experience in war. War has matured him and changed his attitudes to his sweetheart, Marta de Soria, who is consistently more interested in the Falange than in Ignacio. Meditation and an encounter with his first sweetheart, Ana María, lead Ignacio to accept the fact that his love for Marta no longer exists. He breaks with her, resumes with Ana María, and renews their idyll of romantic, adolescent love begun so many years before on the beaches of San Feliü de Guíxols. Love, however, brings problems. Since Ana María is the daughter of an aristocrat, Ignacio is accused of being a social climber. This problem is left for its solution in Gironella's next volume of the series, tentatively entitled *Los hombres lloran solos* (*Men Cry Alone*). The romantic episodes between Ignacio and Ana María are sweet, sentimental and empty although Ignacio's break with Marta is written with great delicacy and some psychological insight. Ignacio's argument when he ends their engagement forms one of Gironella's most sustained and forceful prose passages in the entire work:

I don't know how to tell you. Words are useless. I've fought, fought for weeks. . . . I've come to the conclusion that we wouldn't be happy, that we'd be making an irreparable error. . . . Please don't believe I deceived you. . . . Because I know that you've always loved me very much and I have stolen part of your youth. But I finally decided to see you in order to talk to you with all due frankness. It's better that we break our engagement, Marta . . .[4]

In Ignacio's new-found freedom, he turns to reflection on life, love, and war. He becomes a fervent opponent of war if it means fighting Communism on foreign soil. He prefers to rebuild Spain rather than to kill Communists. Mateo Santos' willingness to fight Communism and lead a Spanish Blue Division into Russia disturbs him and widens an opening breach that began years before when he and Ignacio differed as to Falange policy. Ignacio believes his best friend (and brother-in-law) is immature and unrealistic. Mateo, however, is no longer Ignacio's problem since his fate is now joined to that of Pilar.

The Peace Has Broken Out is devoted to Pilar's marriage to Mateo and the birth of their son, César Santos Alvear. Although the recital of their postwar reunion, their vows, their decisions on matrimony and political obligation are carefully detailed, they are episodic and obviously predictable. Unpredictable, however, is Mateo's fanatical idealism and willingness to sacrifice his life and family to the fight against Communism. Pilar, unsuccessfully, resorts to tears to dissuade Mateo from action. When he refuses, she withdraws within herself to become a war wife, dependent upon her family for emotional support. She is not the Pilar of strength and courage in adversity. She is a weak and weeping bourgeoise.

Her cousin Paz is the new woman of Spain, progressive, adventurous, indomitable—an incarnation of the reconstruction. Paz has two principles: love and Communism. Her Communism estranges her from Pilar and the Alvear family. (The Alvears are pro-Falange.) Paz's amorous conquests, especially the episode with Pachín, center forward of Gerona's soccer team, are more interesting than her political activities. She is sensual, exciting, and for her each new day is an exploration and a discovery of herself. As yet, Gironella's treatment of Paz Alvear and her romantic life is inconclusive. Paz, however, shows a vigor and strength differing from most Gironellan heroes and heroines who are reduced to sentimental "romantic" attitudes.

Many new characters enter the flow of *The Peace Has Broken Out*, and they represent new situations for the Alvears as for Spain. Dr. Chaos exemplifies, even to his name, a relative novelty in Spanish fiction—mental perturbation resultant from his active homosexuality. Manuel Fontana is a renowned lawyer to whom Ignacio is apprentice. Manuel and his wife Esther find a happiness in marriage Ignacio hopes to find when eventually he marries Ana María. The new bishop, Gregorio Lascasas, cultivated and respected, is the revivified Catholic Church and works for the renewal of Spain with the new governor to help Gerona through its period of reconstruction. In Padre Forteza, the renascent Church again aids the Alvears to adjust to César's death and he is the active exponent within the Church for his beatification. New characters, too numerous for anything but summary identification, crowd Gironella's canvases. They enter and leave the world of the Alvears.

The destinies of some of the characters of the two earlier Civil War novels widen with a Spain whose horizons are expanding. Thus, Julio García, after Paris and London, attempts to adjust to Washington, D.C. at the conclusion of *The Peace Has Broken Out*. Letters to the Alvears from Cosme Vila maintain his continuity. Cosme Vila, in Moscow, is with *El Responsable*, attending classes in communism and ever faithful to the Party Line. David and Olga Pol, still active in communism, have fled to Mexico to become fairly successful publishers. Thus, Gironella's purposive dispersals of his characters allow them to serve as mirrors for his international engagements involving Spain. Again, Ignacio meets Canela, an adolescent "love," in the streets of Toulouse. (He had been recalled to Army Service to help the new governor cope with espionage and the problems of Spanish refugees.) On duty in France, he meets Canela, ill and dispirited and alone. She can provide Ignacio, however, with news of his cousin José. José has become a gigolo and lives with a well-known brothel madam in Toulouse. Other secondary characters also appear through the working of fortuitous coincidence, usually to be dismissed in an occasional chapter or even in a few lines.

Incidentally, Eloy, the war orphan introduced in *One Million Dead* as an adopted member of the Alvear family, might have been expected to play a major part in this sequel, but his role is here peripheral and superficial. His passion for sports and soccer is his only quality of importance. This failure to develop Eloy may well be Gironella's slip in construction but it may also be possible that the author is saving him as a major character when he has arrived at an interesting state of maturity. His role may well be developed later in this series. If so, Gironella has maintained a continuity in keeping this character alive.

Upon the Alvears focuses all primary action in *The Peace Has Broken Out*. The revelation of their story gives this novel what interest it possesses. Unfortunately, the Alvears are not so interesting in themselves as in the earlier volumes. All too often their reactions are predictable. Gironella had failed to utilize to advantage his "fusion" of history and fiction.

Peace has its preconceived pattern from which it does not

swerve. National events open key chapters reported as headlines from Gerona's newspaper *Amanecer* and the townspeople discuss international events. (Such problems as Spain in World War II provide most of the conversation and argument of the Café Nacional, formerly the Café Neutral.) The Alvear family comes into discussion, both as a group and separately. Occasional chapters discuss Gerona, the passage of the seasons, holiday celebrations, religious festivals, and political rallies, but the cycle always returns to national events, and Spanish regeneration. The two-year period of *Peace* comes full circle every six months and Gironella never varies this pattern. Consequently, his intrigues are unexciting and tame since international events are really peripheral. Gironella may have his opportunty to dramatize history but his characterization has no real freedom. Clearly, Gironella's "fusion" does not fit this volume. The two years 1939-41 (the first years of peace), have no urgency nor power for direct reaction upon individuals. In fact, characters have too much free time to meditate and prefer thought to action. The novel is slow, relaxed, even paced, to be continued in Volume Four.

Gironella is careful to incorporate new major influences affecting Spain. In this volume they are the appeal of the Axis powers for Franco to become an ally, and the rise of a constellation of corporate structures. They are not thoroughly integrated with the fictional concerns of the characters.

The Peace Has Broken Out ends with the birth of Pilar's son César, perhaps symbolically the rebirth of the murdered César Alvear, candidate for heroic sanctity.

Since Gironella gives to his characters little new insight into themselves, it is reasonable to assume further continuations will be as verbose and episodic. Although *Peace* lies well in the tradition of the generation novel, it lacks the sweep and vitality of Gironella's earlier war novels, nor does it compare with its great predecessors of the nineteenth century.

II *Appraisal of the Trilogy*

The Cypresses Believe in God is Gironella's best novel. Its happy balance between history and fiction synthesizes an organic and full-scale portrait of prewar Spain. *One Million Dead* is less

successful for its concentrates too heavily both on the theme of
death and somewhat heavy-handed historical documentation.
The Peace Has Broken Out, however, is even less successful. His
optimism and advocacy of life (as compared even with *One
Million Dead*), its characters and situations lack both spontaneity
and the ring of truth. Thus, such harmony as *The Cypresses*
achieves, less successful in *One Million Dead*, is not recaptured
in *Peace* because the latter novel relies too heavily on fictional
contrivances and its many banal situations for its action. Volumes
One and Two clearly stand as independent creations but each is
a necessary liaison for *Peace*. Although Gironella is true to his
principles and introduces the international theme, widening
horizons for a modern Spain, and the careful rendition of specific
local situations, these qualities are without sensible effect on the
impact of *The Peace Has Broken Out*. Their inclusion is fortunate
but not decisive. Nevertheless, Gironella in *Peace* sets in motion
a host of new characters upon which to draw in the future. A
clear realist prose, skill in dialogue, and occasional sharp insights
seem frustrated. *Peace* suffers from his lack of spontaneous inspiration. Even more serious, the actions of the Alvears are
external descriptions and do not seem to flow from necessity.
Incident, often coincidental, causes a change in position of his
characters.

Gironella in his original intention embarked upon an explanation of Spain, the Civil War, and himself. His success opened to
him new possibilities, and the very fact that Spain continues
gave him an occasion to develop these two first novels. This
ambitious possibility offers a perennial and ever-present background for a generation novel. Unfortunately, Gironella has not
succeeded as yet in integrating his original purpose and this
projection, now infinitely extended, does not reflect the actions
of his characters. He is faced with a fundamental problem of
integration. *Peace* does not indicate that he has met his challenge.
Its seven hundred-odd pages are unlikely to increase meaning-
fully the reputation he has already achieved. Continuations, possibly, may be more fortunate.

CHAPTER 13

Latest Works

I *Gironella Returns to the Essay*

AS this book was going to press, José María Gironella published
two new works: *Gritos del mar* (*Shouts from the Sea*) and
En Asia se muere bajo las estrellas (*In Asia You Die Under the
Stars*). Gironella's *Shouts* is a series of articles previously published in numerous Spanish magazines and newspapers between
1952 and 1967. It follows the trajectory of his earlier books of
essays such as *Persons, Ideas and Seas,* offering a miscellany of
ideas and thoughts on numerous themes, which occasionally enlighten the reader. Similarly, *Asia* is another of his travel books
written in the same journalistic style as *Shouts*. Like its predecessor, *Japan and Her Ghosts*, it describes Gironella's third trip to
Asia utilizing his gift for journalistic prose. Neither volume advances the author's career; rather, they confirm Gironella's capable use of the essay to describe himself and the world around
him.

Shouts from the Sea is a long work of 516 pages. It consists of
ten separate divisions in which Gironella has included a wide
range of essays on a variety of subjects under such titles as
"Diverse Meditations," "Spanish Themes," "On Modern Art,"
"Travel Experiences," "The Turbulent Twentieth Century," "A
Polemic about Doctors," "Suggestions," "Religious Themes,"
"Political Themes," and "Interviews." In one of these, he tells us
that *Shouts* is a "series of chronicles on a wide range of subject
matter."[1] His audience is "the man in the street, the common
man."[2] His writings are "not only an echo, but a shout. His mis-
sion . . . is to expose his subject on the pages of a newspaper."[3]
Evidently, Gironella's intellectual curiosity plus a desire to interpret and change the world around him are the motives behind
these essays. Although Gironella does not explain exactly what

157

changes should be made, his articles investigate problematic situations and let the reader react to these thoughts.

In his prologue, Gironella recognizes the "heterogeneous nature" of his essays. He says they form "a mosaic with one common melody—[his] preoccupation with everything that affects the life of contemporary man."[4] At once Gironella's sincerity, seriousness of purpose, and progressive maturity as a consequence of his experiences show clearly in a reading of these essays. Occasionally, Gironella's logic in the development of his thought is apparent, even though a reader may not always agree with his conclusions.

In the section, "Diverse Meditations," the most interesting essays deal with Gironella's art of writing and his personal life. "La necesidad de escribir" ("The Need to Write") expresses his atavistic drive to *vaciarse* or communicate with his public. He sees himself as the spokesman of all writers seeking to create. Yet, in his quest for self-expression, Gironella admits in another essay that "No sabemos nada" ("We Know Nothing"). "Publicity invades us and the quantity of information we have clouds our minds and disorients us."[5] Gironella constantly looks for reliable facts and, in the past, utilized valid historical documents as the basis of his Civil War novels. However, he now considers such documents to be "fragments of the truth," and doubts the validity of all information.

In a letter to José María Pemán, Gironella admits that his life experiences are the source of his writing. In fact, he wrote *Phantoms of My Brain* as a consequence of his own personal suffering. Description of his nervous breakdown was a form of catharsis, of liberation. Gironella says he strives for a peaceful spirit in the essay "Paz en su corazón" ("Peace in His Heart") and feels in "Soy hombre, río y lloro" ("I Am a Man, I Laugh, I Cry") that happiness is more than mere satisfaction of appetites in today's spiritually drifting world. At times the author looks for spiritual solace to Catholicism as he commemorates the miracle of birth in his essay, "Carta a un niño recién nacido" ("Letter to a Recently Born Child"). He stresses the values of being a separate individual, eclectic but not an imitation, in "Seamos hermanos, pero no Siameses" ("Let's Be Brothers, Not Siamese Twins"). Stressing the necessity for individuality, Gironella reiterates his plea for internationalism in another essay on this theme. He realizes it is almost impossible to achieve this goal, "an abstraction more remote than the conquest of Mars,"[6] but does not despair in his struggle. In his essay "Patriotismo" ("On Patriotism"), Gironella praises the Common Market, foresees the end of chauvinism, and predicts the development of a common language, fair trade, and equality throughout the world.

Gironella is the advocate of change. He recognizes his own need for travel in "La diversión no es un juego" ("Diversion Is Not a Game"). One of his essays, "Juego con los números" ("Playing with Numbers"), is an exploration of numbers and their statistical relevance based upon Gironella's abilities at free association—certainly a divertissement that should not be taken too seriously. On the other hand, "La huída, signo de la época" ("Flight, Sign of an Epoch") is a devastating treatise on man's evasion of daily life in the twentieth century, a theme he took up so capably in his book of short stories, *We Are All Fugitives*.

In "Nuestra responsabilidad" ("Our Responsibility"), Gironella discusses racism and its remedies. He concludes that our notions of justice and love are the basis of our desire for equality among all the races. However, Gironella is at his best when he describes his youth in Gerona. His essay, "Nuestra ciudad, nuestra memoria" ("Our City, Our Memory"), is a literary evocation in praise of his birthplace. He is shaken quickly from nostalgia when he considers, in "Trampa para incautos" ("Trap for the Gullible") and in "En cuanto a la violencia" ("On Violence"), the problem of crime in Spain. In the first essay, he notes Spain's predisposition to violence as a consequence of its historical and artistic heritage: its tradition of the picaresque, its black humor, its *arte goyesca* and *tremendismo* or stressing the horrific. In the second essay, he condemns Spanish television for the great number of programs showing violence, and prefers that the viewer seek examples of more positive values, such as love and faith.

Returning to contemplate his own career, Gironella concludes his "Diverse Meditations" with an essay entitled "La novela, ¿género agotado?" ("The Novel, Exhausted Genre?"). Because the human mind is always an enigma, Gironella believes that the novelist can endlessly explore the infinite possibilities of thought and behavior. "For human thoughts continue to be a mystery and the novelist can gain access into them, perhaps even more so than the psychiatrist."[7] Thus, Gironella does not view the novel as a dead genre, but as one replete with future possibilities. "The novel is life and life never wears itself out."[8] He warns us, however, that the novel is an arduous genre and expert novelists are few. He believes this literary form will be resuscitated by young, capable writers, who are "the catalysts, witnesses of the individual's journey through life in the vast context of society."[9]

Gironella's section of "Spanish Themes" contains no less than sixteen essays of which at least half are worthwhile journalism. "El hombre español y el diálogo" ("The Spaniard and Conversation") contains a good description of the contemporary Spaniard's mentality. Gironella believes the Spaniard does not argue ideas, but convictions. He cannot discuss problems for their own sake or to discover the truth, but merely to prove that he is right. Egotism and the Spaniard's driving determination to win an argument are far more important factors than objectivity. Gironella declares that Spaniards are not logical, but temperamental people. He points out their desire for prolixity and blames this trait for the country's isolationism. His view of Spain's future is pessimistic because of the Spaniard's egoistic preference for monologue instead of for meaningful dialogue.

Gironella is equally critical in the essay, "¿Es feminino el pueblo español?" ("Are the Spanish People Feminine?"). He says Spain is a "feminine country" because it insists on an agricultural economy. "The ideal of feminine towns is to live, not to progress."[10] When Spain becomes an industrial nation, it will be masculine. In "Gerona, ciudad bombardeada" ("Gerona, Bombed-Out City"), he continues his declamation against Spaniards and their society. Gironella criticizes his birthplace because it has not kept pace with Spain's development since the Civil War. Gerona is like a bombed-out city: static, paralyzed, inert. In contrast, Gerona is portrayed lovingly in an article from a travel book, *La España en cada provincia* (*Spain in Each Province*). Gironella demonstrates the charms of his native city, encouraging tourism and welcoming beneficial changes that progressively make Gerona the "gem of Catalonia." These two articles about Gerona are written with sustained interest and serious intent. They demonstrate Gironella's love of Catalonia and respect for her traditions. They are tributes to the past as well as to the future of Gerona and her citizens. The spirit of commemoration is common to most of the essays in this section, especially "La muerte puede ser un pseudónimo" ("Death Can Be a Pseudo-nym"), Gironella's tribute to the life and spirit of Azorín. Gironella cannot resist an opportunity to discuss his fascination with the theme of death. Our author views death as "the absolute experience" that defies explanation. "Death is the supreme paradox, the irrational moment. Death has always been compared to winter . . . life is warmth."[11]

In "Modesto homenaje a un amigo de Asia" ("A Modest Tribute to a Friend from Asia"), Gironella praises Luis María Ansón, Asian correspondent of *ABC*, Madrid's leading daily newspaper, for his tenacity and daring in covering the Vietnam newsfront. He describes Ansón as "a powerful mind with a hunger for knowledge; a talented journalist who defies the popular contention that Spain is a country full of frustrated talents."[12] (Gironella will take up in detail his adventures with Ansón and his wife, Beatrice, in his third travel volume on Asia when he discusses the war in Vietnam.)

Gironella continues his praises of Catalonia with "La Federació de Joves Cristians de Catalunya" ("The Federation of Young Christians of Catalonia"). He says, "this organization taught me to love God, which in turn filled my own thirst for transcendence. It brought me to a love of the intellect, and a belief that man's thought is the most noble of all creations. I came to love my family . . . , my friends . . . , my birthplace . . . , my freedom."[13] Gironella recalls his participation in this organization at the beginning of the Civil War. The recent death of its leader, Félis Millet Maristany, prompts the tribute and casts our author into reflection: "He taught me about life . . . and in moments of personal crisis, the Federation saved me from acts of intemperance and desperation."[14] This important essay reveals another influence that shaped the author's mind.

Gironella completes this section with an indictment against the Spaniard's indifference in "Sobre la falta de curiosidad de los españoles" ("On the Spaniard's Lack of Curiosity"). He maintains there will always be a nucleus of enlightened Spaniards, but recognizes widespread illiteracy and the dangerous appeal of television to the ignorant masses. Spaniards need perspective, and Gironella makes his plea for international travel and student exchange in this serious, but somewhat disjointed article.

The author's two essays in the section "On Modern Art" demonstrate he may know very little about the worth or meaning of this genre, but can appraise it in his own terms. He concludes after reviewing an exhibition of the Catalan artist Antonio Taipés, that "the more ambiguity in an artist's work, the greater will be his success."[15] Gironella dislikes the "new paintings" and the contemporary artists' tendency to imitate one another. In another lengthy article, "Hablemos otra vez ¡ay! del arte moderno" ("Let's Speak Again, Ay! about Modern Art"), Gironella presents a systematic attack on modern art, but makes the following worthwhile conclusions. He believes that the key to artistic creation is authenticity. Pedantry, propaganda, and crass materialism stifle true art.

Of the ten sections of Gironella's *Shouts from the Sea*, one of the most interesting is his "Travel Experiences." Nine articles contained herein are fragments of previously published works. An exception is a beautifully written, journalistic piece entitled "Curaçao—admirable fundación holandesa en el Caribe" ("Curaçao, Admirable Dutch Colony in the Caribbean"). Gironella's visit to the island generates an unending love for this marvelous Dutch colony. Rivaling this affection for Curaçao is his homage to "Finlandia, país humilde y sereno" ("Finland, Humble and Peaceful Country"). The author discovers an entirely new world and serenity in this cold northern land. He supports the observations of Angel Ganivet in the latter's *Cartas Finlandesas* (*Finnish Letters*), but finds one discordant note—the religious indifference of the Finns. Gironella says their lack of belief in God leads to spiritual starvation, existential and anguished emptiness, desperation, and suicide. Nevertheless, Finland is one of the most fascinating travel experiences of his lifetime.

A curious addition to *Shouts from the Sea* is his essay, "Un cauce para la agresividad" ("A Release for Aggressions"). While visiting a factory in the city of Osaka, Gironella is impressed by the owner's guile. His employees are permitted to pommel a rubber doll that looks like him, consequently releasing their aggressions. Gironella attributes this practice to Japan's atavistic belief in representations, the exact significance of masks, and the latent aggressiveness of the Japanese character. He speculates upon the advantages of such a release in contrast to our Western society where we level our aggressions at someone or something real and hurt ourselves in the process.

The remaining articles in this section are of little significance —a short tribute to Nikos Kazantsakis, a minor divertissement on wax museums, a visit to a wine cellar in Gerona and the reprinting of his introduction to a book of photographs about the "turbulent" twentieth century. They indicate the author's gift for writing expository prose on a variety of minor matters.

However, *Shouts from the Sea* does gather its emotional (if not intellectual) momentum from Gironella's polemic against a group of doctors. At the outset, Gironella admits his profound respect and reverence for the medical profession in "Estamos indefensos" ("We Are Defenseless"); but in his "Carta a los médicos" ("Letter to Doctors"), he criticizes the perversion of their ideals and their worship of materialism. In reply to many doctors outraged by Gironella's attack, our author vindicates himself in a long article, "Medicina de ricos, medicina de pobres" ("Medicine for the Rich, Medicine for the Poor"), in which Gironella stresses the different treatment of patients as a consequence of their incomes. In the same article, he presents an historical view of the medical profession since Greek times and hopes the fundamental position of the "ethical" doctor will not change. Medicine, like the priesthood, should be an art of love, a compassionate inclination towards the masses without anticipation of material gain. In a final burst of energy, Gironella replies to a letter attacking his use of psychological theories in *Woman, Arise and Walk!* and his personal accounts of psychic experiences in *Phantoms of My Brain*. Gironella defends his right of literary license to depict a psychiatrist as a symbol of God, and his freedom to describe vividly his years of nervous suffering during a state of mental breakdown.

Sometimes, Gironella's *Shouts* reverberate and at other times they are merely empty cries lost in silence. For example, defense of his literary creations is unnecessary, but Gironella fans the flames of polemics, adding fuel to the fire, often apparently just to keep his name in print. Although his *Shouts* contains some major problems that deserve an author's consideration, there are many minor ones in his section, "Suggestions," that are of little value.

"Barcelona y el templo de la unidad cristiana" ("Barcelona and the Temple of Christian Unity") is his plea for international religious unity; "Cataluña debe hacer algo" ("Catalonia Ought to Do Something") was written in appreciation of Carlos Buigas' luminous fountains in Montjuich Park and for Antonio Gaudí and his still uncompleted Church of the Sacred Family. Gironella appeals to fellow Catalans to patronize their own artists and to support "sound and light" spectacles in Barcelona. Gironella's suggestions for world-wide Christianity and internationalism are repeated in those sections containing his essays on religious and political themes. In fact, the majority of these ten essays echo thoughts already expressed in *Persons, Ideas and Seas* and *Japan and Her Ghosts*. Our interest in Gironella's travels, however, is reinforced by two essays: "Al habla con los Jesuitas de Bombay" ("Talking with Jesuits in Bombay") and "Misioneros catalanes en Bombay" ("Catalan Missionaries in Bombay"). Gironella gives his motives for interviews with priests. They are wise and saintly, excellent guides in foreign countries and above all, because of their ecclesiastical authority, they have access to cultural centers and otherwise inaccessible places of interest. A frustrated novice himself, Gironella's personal concern for Catalan priests in foreign places is a projection of his own unfulfilled aspirations. He enjoys speculating on their personal lives and their acceptance abroad. Gironella proselytes his notion of Catholicism when he discusses the meaning of intransigence in "Palabras que causan un estupor" ("Words That Cause a Stupor"), the role of faith in "¿Ama o no ama Dios a todos los hombres?" ("Does God Love Or Not Love All Men?") and the need for evangelization in "También en el Japón ocurren milagros" ("Miracles Also Occur in Japan").

His political views presented in five essays are also repetitions of thoughts expressed in longer works, such as those in his book, *On China and Cuba*. Gironella's fascination with the lives and practices of dictators is the theme of a somewhat eclectic article documenting the published works of Lenin, Mussolini, Mao Tse-tung, Hitler, and Stalin for the author believes all dictators assume their roles because they soon become aware of their destinies. They are "prophets" of the people who cause "seismic commotions," usually for destructive purposes. Gironella views all dictators, including Fidel Castro, as "gesticulatory figures, demagogues that inspire resentment and fear."[16]

Gironella's anti-Communist views have been discussed in Chapter 10 of this book. Again, in his *Shouts*, he protests against communism in "Roma y su plagario—el comunismo" ("Rome and Its Plague—Communism") and in "A la escucha del comunismo" ("Listening to Communism"). The first article is a condemnation of Italian Communists and Masons who subscribe to this religion of obedience and hate which is antithetical to Catholic teachings. The second article is notable because it reverses Gironella's stand on the European Common Market. Since Spain did not achieve entry, Gironella now calls it a "violent abscess," attributing its creation to Communist influence. He predicts its demise because the Common Market is rooted in "instincts contrary to man's nature—freedom, unrestrained progress in commerce, etc."[17] The author's last two articles on politics are denunciations of the United States: "Paradojas de los Estados Unidos" ("Paradoxes of the United States") demonstrates Gironella's stereotyped views of American society. In "Occidente, pese a las diferencias, está básicamente unido . . . y dispuesto" ("The Western World, in Spite of Its Differences, Is Basically United and Genteel"), Gironella uses the brutal killing of Robert F. Kennedy as his point of departure to condemn all political assassinations and seeks reaffirmation of positive political values to defend life and liberty.

Gironella's last section of his *Shouts* is a group of essays based upon interviews with two university professors, a doctor of neurosurgery, his psychiatrist, and an ophthalmologist. His "Teoría del hombre nuevo" ("Theory of the New Man") is Gironella's attempt to comprehend Dr. Arturo Fernández-Cruz's view of modern man as a product of new scientific methods, and of industrial and technological advances that have shaped today's world. Gironella discusses modern man's refutation of nature and the negative aspects of his "new" life—envy, anger, anguish, insecurity, lack of individuality, mental illness. His hopes for Spain's continued material progress parallel to its technological advances is reaffirmed despite the aforementioned detrimental factors.

His interview with Dr. Adolfo Ley in "El mundo de neurocirugía" ("The World of Neurosurgery") reinforces Gironella's personal fascination with infra-sensorial perception, dream states, amnesia, morality, and conscience. "El mundo del psiquiatra" ("The World of the Psychiatrist"), particularly his personal psychiatrist, Dr. Ramón Vidal Teixidor, is Gironella's rambling exploration into social psychiatry and the art and the dangers of using tranquilizers. His "Conversación con el doctor don Enrique Salgado" ("Conversation with Dr. Enrique Salgado") documents Gironella's bizarre interest in myopia. This essay is a personal tribute to Salgado and to his theories. It also contains a listing of world famous myopes that supposedly forms the nucleus of a "superior race" because of faulty vision. The general impression after reading these interviews is Gironella's personal wonder and at times bewilderment before these men who are established authorities in areas beyond the mentality and training of the author. These essays are testimony to his hero worship. Gironella is an inquiring reporter in quest of information, not an expert interviewer. He relates what is relevant to further the reader's knowledge, but is a layman before the distinguished professional.

II   *Evaluation of* Shouts from the Sea

It is difficult to reach conclusions after reading *Shouts from the Sea.* Taking up this volume, a reader will discover a potpourri of essays, a plethora of ideas, some valuable, others unworthy of consideration. The reader must select personally those essays which are of interest to him. Although Gironella's *Shouts* is strictly journalistic prose, it is occasionally revitalized by an appealing personal point of view. It was stressed earlier that his *Shouts* are fragmentary thoughts previously discussed in depth in earlier sustained works. His audience is still the general reader. Although there is very little that is new thematically in this collection of essays, we respect Gironella's right to express his opinions on diverse matters: "I have written thick volumes on controversial themes. The balance of my labor could be summed up in the following way: the man on the street, the *vox populi* argues. I argue myself about the literary quality of what I write. On the other hand, nobody can refute my sincerity. I say what I feel, I'll always say it. And I assume the responsibility for my words. That is the only badge that I can show to my readers."[18] His sincerity in appraising fairly a variety of subjects is the common denominator of the diverse essays contained in *Shouts from the Sea.*

III   *Gironella's Third Asian Journey*

The second new work, *In Asia You Die Under the Stars*, has

a rather poetic title for a notebook of fiercely realistic, intensely personal impressions of Gironella's travels through Thailand, Vietnam, Formosa, the Philippines, Hong Kong, Macao, Cambodia, and India. The title refers to the Vietnamese war: "Vietnam vomited blood; it was dying. Vietnam was dying under the stars."[19]

Asia is a straightforward journalistic prose work similar in many respects to *Japan and Her Ghosts* and *Persons, Ideas and Seas*. Gironella wrote it for the average Spaniard seeking timely information about the Orient and its problems. Intentionally didactic, *Asia* also presents Gironella's personal impressions of the Orient through the eyes of a Spaniard in order to promote Spanish tourism. It was published by Plaza and Janes as part of their "Around the World in Eighty Books" series. It is a handsome volume, augmented by over one hundred photographs taken by the author. In this respect, it is superior to his earlier travel books.

Each of *Asia's* eight chapters presents Gironella's thoughts on arrival, his problems of adjustment, scenic tours, personal interviews, historical and political discussions, and departures from the eight lands under scrutiny. "We closed our eyes and listened to the powerful noise of the plane's motors. The plane was a live being, capable of leaping from one country to another, saving us tremendous distances without causing psychological traumas."[20] Although this quotation appears at the end of Gironella's trajectory through Asia, it is suitable to begin his series of adventures in the Orient. Gironella's journalistic style is appropriate to this travel work. In *Asia*, the reader has the sensation of travelling with the author, of actually seeing what the writer sees, and of being submerged with him in the ways of life and in the cultures that he analyzes and observes. Here, again, *Asia* is superior to its predecessors. Gironella is more personal, digresses less, and maintains relatively objective postures before the events he witnesses. With this work, Gironella hoped to fill the void of scant bibliography on the Orient in the Spanish language, and to present a clear, concise view of Asia's current problems.

In his prologue, Gironella cannot understand his personal fascination for the Orient: "My interior javelin fell in Asia and it remained stuck there. I fell in love with Asia just as there are souls that fall in love with a cross. Because Asia is this: a cruci-

fied continent—although the wood of its cross smells of sandalwood and appears painted with lively colors."[21] Gironella admittedly strives for authenticity and leaves the reader free to
judge the value of *Asia* for himself. His primary interest is to
express what he saw, heard and felt on this third trip to the
Orient with his wife, Magda.

Our intention in reviewing *Asia* is *not* to outline Gironella's
diverse impressions in each of the eight cities he visited—a Gargantuan task. After reading the entire work, we believe only four
of its eight chapters are worthy of comment: his impressions of
Saigon (Vietnam), the second city he visited on his itinerary,
Phnom Penh (Cambodia), Bangkok (Thailand), and Calcutta
(India), his last stop before returning to Barcelona via Rome.
These chapters are valuable reporting because they contain
emotionally moving observations of well-known international
problems. His Vietnamese and Indian experiences, particularly,
differ widely from the large bulk of anecdotal and personal material in other chapters. This type of material provides continuity
for the reader but contains few profound or enlightening thoughts.

A. *Vietnam*

In Chapter Two, Gironella and his wife are met at Saigon's
airport by Dang Manh-chuan, a Vietnamese reporter working for
Newsweek Magazine. They settle into their rooms at the Hotel
Majestic in downtown Saigon and shortly after are contacted by
a Spanish correspondent for *ABC*, Luis María Ansón, author of
El grito del oriente (*Cry from the Orient*), and his wife, Beatrice.
Both couples tour Saigon during Gironella's first day there and
observe the heavy French colonial influence, the chaotic, teeming
population of the city, the presence of United States soldiers,
and the effects of the war itself:

The Vietnamese war is a war of helicopters. Helicopters of all types.
A soldier who is wounded on the front, wherever he is, is picked up
a short while after by helicopter and taken to a hospital, and later, by
plane to the United States. On the other hand, the Vietcong guerrillas
often fight under terrible conditions; crouched in their huts, breathing
fresh air by means of a bamboo shoot. And the guerrillas can last
years and years. The Vietcong defend their own; they are frantic and
as I told you concerning the psychological aspect, the Americans
commit striking errors, not only with respect to the civilian population but also with the South Vietnamese politics, their allies.[22]

Gironella tours Saigon by night and sees the mortar bursts in the city. Apart from side trips to a modern pagoda, various temples, botanical gardens, and zoos, he also visits the slums of Saigon, the rubber forests, a Saigon restaurant, a brothel, and, later, attends Sunday mass in Saigon's cathedral. He believes the South Vietnamese completely ignore the threat of communism, Mao Tse-tung's power, and the significance of the war going on around them. Gironella blames the Vietnamese war on Churchill, Roosevelt, and de Gaulle. Their victories precipitated the surrender of half of Europe and now, half of Asia to communism. Gironella, himself, finds communism an unsatisfactory solution to any problem, wherever the locality.

Although Gironella digresses occasionally into discussions of Vietnamese poetry, the significance of Catholicism in Southeast Asia, the efforts of Spanish doctors in the Vietnam war, an interview with a captured Vietcong prisoner and later, the family of his journalist friend, Dang Manh-chuan, Gironella comes to a series of painful conclusions: "... the American's presence in Vietnam, like Chiang Kai-shek's in Formosa, is indispensable in order to prevent Mao's avalanche in Asia. If the Americans abandon Vietnam and Formosa, all of Southeastern Asia will fall at one time into the hands of Mao Tse-tung."[23] After spending ten days in Saigon, Gironella concludes his thoughts on the Vietnam War. Here he contradicts his previous statement on the United States' position in Southeast Asia. He believes the United States lacks leadership in its foreign policy in Southeast Asia. The United States does not have the elasticity or the maturity required to evaluate the problems of other continents. Although the Americans insist on the "democratic way of life" and support the war financially, they will not be able to keep Southeast Asia from communism. Even if the Americans leave, they will not bring peace to Vietnam. Gironella predicts Southeast Asia's complete surrender to communism, an ideology synonymous with constant and well-disciplined warfare.

B. *Cambodia*

The Hotel Royal in Phnom Penh is Gironella's first stop in Cambodia. He first interviews the Spanish Ambassador, Don José Varela, who organizes for him an expedition into the forests and ancient cities around the capital. Travelling by car, Gironella and his wife are fascinated by the *stupas* (funeral monuments), and exquisite Buddhist temples where they witness the ritual shaving of the heads of newly ordained monks. Although usually a dispassionate spectator, Gironella at times reports some of his personal emotions. He smokes opium and feels a wonderful "sensation of peace"—a sensation greater than any caused by barbiturates or electroshock treatments.

The remaining section of this chapter provides us with Gironella's descriptions of the visual delights of Angkor, the capital of the Kmer Empire. Gironella tells of the origin, historical development, and decadence of Angkor: its Brahman influences, its typical "Cambodian" architectural character, and its incredibly huge reconstructed statues on the Avenue of Giants, a group of thirty stone figures of Buddhist gods three times the height of an average human being. At times, the only opportunity Gironella has to see these monuments in and around Angkor is to travel through dense forests by elephant. He describes his feelings while riding atop an elephant: nausea and kidney pains. Apart from Gironella's persistent, hilarious battles with mosquitoes, these elephant trips provide some of the few humorous episodes in the book. Returning to a serious mood, Gironella is deeply impressed by the intense fatalism of Cambodia's oriental world. He acknowledges Prince Sihanouk's contributions to the country, especially the perpetuation of a political system based on "patriarchal communism," and admits that Sihanouk governs a peaceful, united nation whose people have all the freedoms they would enjoy under a monarchy.

C. *Thailand*

Gironella next journeys to Bangkok, a city which invites comparison to Phnom Penh. Bangkok, unlike Phnom Penh, is one of the far eastern cities willing to accept American aid in exchange for United States military bases. Except for some evidence of French culture, Phnom Penh appeared untouched by colonialism. Bangkok, however, is overrun by American influence. Gironella quickly dismisses these evidences of a foreign power and investigates the authentic "Thai character." Travelling by motorboat along the Chao Pya River, Gironella is impressed with the great number and infinite variety of Buddhist temples, especially the Dawn Pagoda whose *stupas* remind him of spires of Western cathedrals. He never resists an opportunity to discuss religion and its contributions to society. He is mystified by Buddhism and the concept of Nirvana, yet delights in the temples dedicated to Buddha. However, his own bias is evident in his feelings of triumph at the conversion of many Buddhists to Catholicism.

Gironella sincerely admires the people of Thailand because they love peace, nature, are contemplative, and prefer the genuine to the artificial. The "smiling Thais" are well known for their tolerance, pacifist attitudes, lack of racial discrimination, and total disregard for caste systems. However, Gironella believes they are dangerous when threatened with loss of honor or independence.

Searching for Spanish influences in Thailand, Gironella discovers Songla, an ancient coastal city founded by Spaniards over four hundred years ago. The Spaniards had originally called it *Señora* because of its physical beauty. It still retains the celebrated Spanish custom of bullfighting. However, bullfighting Thai-style is totally different from the Spanish sport. Two bulls fight each other to the death as the Thais place bets on the possible winner. Gironella admits that this kind of fighting is more natural, but less spectacular, dramatic, and artistic than the sport as practiced in Spain.

Before leaving Thailand, Gironella has an opportunity to visit Bangkok's "floating market"—boats loaded down with all kinds of natural produce: mangos, plantains, coconuts. Another part of the market is on land and contains thousands of stalls displaying native arts, such as hand-tooled ivory *objets d'art* and Cambodian woven goods. Gironella describes this floating market as Bangkok's principal tourist attraction.

Although he enjoys his stay in Bangkok, Gironella is eager to see the suburbs, especially a serpentarium where snakes are kept to collect their venom, used in the manufacture of vaccines and antidotes. Afterwards, he is treated to a typical Thai meal: shark soup, swallow, turtle eggs, and "exquisite" Thailand rice, the most delicious part of the menu according to his admittedly European tastes. Before Gironella leaves Bangkok, he makes one last visit to Lumpini Park which contains a huge statue of Rama I, founder of the city. Gironella is fortunate to witness a "comet fight," a symbolic theatrical representation of the eternal struggle between man and women. The actors are two high-flying kites in the shape of human figures, who battle for dominance of the sky.

Apart from the apparent gaiety of the Thai people, Gironella realizes the proximity of the Vietnam war and the Communist threat to Thailand. The Thai government is anti-Communist, and most officials to whom Gironella spoke believe that the Communist threat is minor. This "ostrich-like" attitude is not unusual for the Thais. They are far from progressive both politically and economically. For example, they prefer using the elephant instead of the tractor.

Gironella ends his stay in Bangkok, the "City of Angels," admiring the beauty and refinement of Thai women at a program of classical dances. He particularly notes their slow tempo, dignified poise and expressive, beautiful hands that afford him an inexplicable aesthetic pleasure of the highest order.

Many of Gironella's Asian experiences reported in this volume give the impression that the author is a traveller, reporting what he sees and feels while "just passing through" from city to city. In Saigon, he is faced with a hot war, and takes a personal stand on the issues. His prose style becomes declamatory, serious, and strongly dramatic. It lapses into journalism and simplifications of thought in Phnom Penh, Bangkok, and in the remainder of his travels until he arrives in Calcutta, an entirely different world from Southeast Asia.

D. *India*

In Calcutta, Gironella reflects upon the misery and the poverty he had previously encountered in Bombay, expecting to see a worse situation here. His initial impressions are worthy of repetition:

... stifling heat, the smell of sandalwood and of tea, naked human flesh ... faces of ashen color, others darker or olive-skinned, skeleton-like turbaned youngsters with legs like sticks ... and the slowness of business transactions, and an exasperating slowness. And the lizards. Lizards on the walls, on the roofs, immobile like the figures on a shield. The fans turned horizontally, demonstrating that everything happens here without the possibility of changing from the supreme norm—that individual and collective existence is a timeless waterwheel for the Indian.[24]

Gironella observes the beggars, ambulatory cases of tuberculosis, and preying vultures flying everywhere. Calcutta is a teeming city that makes him uneasy and nervous. Short visits to the home of the Indian poet Tagore, a planetarium and a park do little to pacify or relieve Gironella's restlessness. He is impressed by the sheer density of the population and points out that India's greatest problem is birth control. Divertissements such as a visit to a Hindu museum and a ballet-music performance by Ravi Shankar's troupe do little to cheer him. A horrible incident, watching an Indian woman, in terrible agony, giving birth to a monstrously deformed foetus on the street, in the midst of indifferent passersby, is one of the most shocking experiences ever witnessed by the Gironellas. Watching the vultures devour a dead old man was equally horrific for them. Although the Gironellas spent only three days in Calcutta, they were emotionally spent and could not wait to return to Spain after two months of travel. Indeed, India deserved a lengthier visit by the Gironellas, but they were not up to it.

IV *Conclusions*

At the end of Gironella's chapter dealing with his travels in Vietnam, Gironella presents his *raison d'être* for the entire travel book: "I am nothing but a tired and tenacious traveller, a simple observer of persons and events with the inalienable right to express through my writings what I think and feel, no matter how painful it may be."[25] *In Asia You Die Under the Stars* is undoubtedly the best of his series of travel books. The writing and style are superior to its predecessors because of tighter organization, fewer personal digressions, and his portrayal of outstanding graphic experiences charged with great emotional impact. Neither *Shouts* nor *Asia* offers new directions to Gironella's career. They are, however, further proof of his literary facility and demonstrate a skillful use of the essay genre to describe multifaceted thoughts and experiences which are essential to Gironella's world.

CHAPTER 14

Gironella's Position and Influence

GIRONELLA feels himself to be "modern man" since his qualities are those of, at once, the man in the street and of the artist. In his best novels his sympathy with the average man shows in leading characters typical of their society and era. The essential nature of the Spaniard for Gironella appears ingenuous without artificiality. He shares with his fellow Spaniards his interest in explaining the complexity of the Civil War and although he does not consider himself superficial, he does intend Spain, with the Alvear family as his creative focus, to be the omnipresent if silent heroine. Such a conception hardly can be confined to the limits of the war novels.[1]

On the other hand, Gironella's career is more than a dedication to *vox populi*. He has produced some complex and stylized works in diverse genres that demand artistic concentration. The short story of Gironella illustrates this point admirably. Gironella is a Catalan of great vital energy and capacity for recuperation and experimentation. His popularity rests on his utilization of personal and universally Spanish experiences to establish, in a slowly developing but real talent, the validity of the singular complex event which dominated his life—the Civil War. His talent is still, even now, in its formative stages.

Although his career is always in a state of flux, Gironella's current literary position is his commitment and his struggles with success and artistic endeavor. His most important works are his first two Civil War novels, but the third, on his earliest theme, the importance of romantic love, is weaker and adds little to his stature in Spanish letters. His first two novels and his most artistic efforts—*We Are All Fugitives* and *Phantoms of My Brain* —are his commercial failures. Gironella's moderately interesting essay-novels, his travel books indicating development of new

174

areas of creativity and personality, have had a mild attraction for the Spanish public and for critical attention. Gironella has been always hesitant to give complete adherence to any ideology for he fears the Spanish public whose support he feels necessary for his career. "I gave lectures in Munich, in Heidelberg, cities visited in former times by the great philosopher-critic Ortega y Gasset. Lecturing where Ortega once lectured was a thought that affected me indescribably. It made me feel like I was a bold charlatan."[2]

Powers of observation and perception and with them his psychological therapy overcame his artistic irresponsibility and convince Gironella they are responsible for his success and his progressive unfolding of latent talents.[3] It may be that his development, as well as sometimes abrupt changes in style and subject matter result from flexibility and individual susceptibility to influence from a dynamic world of ideas. Nevertheless, and although his conscientious artistry and search for improvement in himself and his work cannot be denied, his literary success seems largely due to his revival of the generation novel of the nineteenth century in Spain.

Stylistically, such a revival of realism is a literary anachronism, but his war novels are not unworthy of comparison with such recognized works as Galsworthy's *Forsyte Saga*, Rolland's *Jean Christophe*, Martin du Gard's *Les Thibaults* (*The Thibaults*), Romains' *Les hommes de bonne volonté* (*Men of Good Will*), and Dos Passos' *Manhattan Transfer*. Their popularity is due to the same causes—a panoramic view of their society and a common humanity in characterization. For such reasons, Juan Luis Alborg compares Gironella's realist novels to *Don Quixote*: "If the *Quixote* offers us the most ample and capable vision of Spain in its time associated with the figure of that incredible lunatic, Gironella's vision also affords us a very diverse panorama of contemporary Spain in a manner that informs us through uncommon daring."[4]

Critics dispute Gironella's impartiality, but must accord to him his achievement of an objective panoramic view of Spain for it is this which assures his works their fair degree of political balance. In the traditions of the realist novel, he sets forth publicly his dissatisfaction as in an evocation of these traditions in his greatest success—a focus for the problems of the Spain of his own Civil

War generation. This success is enhanced by his skillful handling of always controversial and sometimes intractable material.

Gironella reinforces nineteenth century concepts by an heroic attempt to widen Spain's intellectual horizons and to speak for the masses as well. He suggests through the creation of the *novela-ensayo* (fictionalized essay) such social and political problems of contemporary Spanish life as exercise Spain's "new wave" novelists, Goytisolo, Delibes, Hortelano, Matute, but without their conscious cultivation of poetic lyricism. Fundamentally, José María Gironella and his work should be viewed as transitional.

Gironella's early career reflects a lack of discipline and feelings of inferiority, but the work of his maturity demonstrates greater cohesiveness and artistry. Gironella's continuing anxiety for popularity may only indicate greater effort to integrate himself and his thematic concerns with the ebb and flow of public demand. It may be, and this must not be overlooked, a recognition of continuing compromise with his artistic standards, and a recognition of an insecurity which takes the form of "always seeking some new thing." The careers of the "popular" writers are too frequently overlooked by Spanish intellectuals despite the positive values that the "popular" artist may consciously or unconsciously exert upon his society. Gironella's travel books and essays have their value because they reflect the taste and help to form the intellectual fashions of the society for which they were written. His works of imagination, "popular" as they too are, result from the dimension of an aesthetic purely personal and individual. Ten years ago, after the publication of *The Cypresses Believe in God*, William J. Grupp analyzed Gironella's work optimistically. It may have some truth today. "It would seem that in the person of José María Gironella, Spain has a novelist of international stature, a man who combines an excellent command and understanding of the novelist's techniques with a clear perception of the spiritual tensions of the world he portrays and the courage to face these tensions realistically and truthfully."[5]

The Peace Has Broken Out, which appeared in October, 1966, is a disappointment, since its more than seven hundred pages is a retrogression to his ingenuous theme of romantic love. It is prolix, episodic, and somewhat banal. Gironella is a perpetual promise but this last novel does not augur too well for new directions or new psychological insight.

Gironella is transitional, still a promise, a question, and Spanish letters must await his evaluation; for Gironella's personal cosmos is continually changing under the dynamic impulses of his talent.

Notes and References

Chapter One

1. Federico Carlos Saínz de Robles provides a schematic outline of these writers in his work, *La novela española en el siglo xx* (Madrid: Ed. Pegaso, 1957), pp. 185–220.
2. Ortega y Gasset discusses the period in his excellent essay, "Ideas sobre la novela," in his *Obras completas* (Madrid: Revista de Occidente, 1947) III, 387–420.
3. Saínz de Robles, p. 227.
4. As reported by I. M. Schevill, "A Day With Gironella," *Hispania,* XLII (May, 1959), 173.
5. Antonio de Hoyos, *Ocho escritores actuales* (Murcia: Aula de Cultura, 1954), p. 59.
6. J. J. Devlin, "Arturo Barea and José María Gironella: Two Interpreters of the Spanish Labyrinth," *Hispania,* XLI (1958), 147.
7. Schevill, p. 174.
8. José María Gironella, *El novelista ante el mundo* (Madrid: Ed. Rialp, 1954), Colección "O crece o muere," No. 52, p. 11.
9. *Idem*
10. *Idem*
11. *Ibid.,* p. 12.
12. *Ibid.,* p. 22.
13. *Idem*
14. *Ibid.,* p. 35.
15. *Ibid.,* p. 8.
16. As expressed by the author in the interview at Arenys de Mar on August 3, 1965.
17. *Idem*
18. A. Kerrigan, "José María Gironella and the Black Legend of Spain," *Books on Trial,* XIV (April-May 1956), 344.

Chapter Two

1. As expressed by the author in the interview at Arenys de Mar on August 3, 1965.
2. *Idem*
3. *Idem*
4. *Idem*
5. *Idem*

6. For an extended discussion of this theme, see Tomás Zamarriego, *Tipología sacerdotal en la novela contemporánea: Bernanos, Mauriac, Gironella* (Madrid: Ed. Razón y fe, 1959).

7. John F. Byrne has translated the author's political essays in *On China and Cuba* (Notre Dame, Indiana: Fides Publishers, 1963).

Chapter Three

1. José Luis Cano in his article "Libros del mes: *Un hombre* de Gironella," *Insula*, XVIII (June 1947), 5, remarks: "Es una sencilla manera de titular una autobiografía."

2. Lawrence H. Klibbe, "Gironella's *Where the Soil Was Shallow*," translation of *Un hombre, Catholic World*, Vol. 188 (Feb. 1959), 401.

3. Gironella, *La marea* (Barcelona: Ed. Planeta, 1947), pp. 375–76.

4. Gironella, *Un hombre* (Barcelona: Ed. Destino, 1946), Colección Ancora y Delfín, Preface.

5. Jacques Barzun, *Classic, Romantic and Modern* (New York: Doubleday-Anchor Books, 1961), p. 94.

6. Gironella, *Un hombre*, p. 16.

7. *Ibid.*, p. 31.

8. *Ibid.*, pp. 147–48.

9. Gironella, *La marea*, p. 8.

10. *Ibid.*, p. 55.

11. Gironella, *Los cipreses creen en Dios* (Barcelona: Ed. Planeta, 1953), p. 298.

12. Gironella, *Mujer, levántate y anda* (Barcelona: Ed. Planeta, 1962), p. ii.

13. *Ibid.*, p. 18.

14. *Ibid.*, p. 123.

Chapter Four

1. José María Gironella, *Los cipreses creen en Dios* (Barcelona: Ed. Planeta, 1953), p. 9.

2. *Ibid.*, p. 11.

3. I. M. Schevill, "A Day With Gironella," *Hispania*, XLII (May 1959), 173.

4. Anthony West, "Books" (Review of *The Cypresses Believe in God*), *New Yorker*, XXXI (May 1955), 120, says: "the writer knows everything there is to know about his characters, their lives, the lives around them and indeed, the essential nature of all creation."

5. Gironella, *Los cipreses*, p. 18.

6. *Ibid.*, p. 19.

7. *Ibid.*, p. 37.

8. José Luis Cano, "Los Libros del mes," *Insula*, Vol. 89 (May 1953), 6.

9. Anthony Kerrigan, "J. M. Gironella and the Black Legend of Spain," *Books on Trial*, XIV, (April-May 1956), p. 343.

10. *Los cipreses*, p. 64.

11. Schevill, *Hispania*, XLII, 174.

12. *Los cipreses*, p. 88.

13. *Ibid.*, p. 117.

14. *Ibid.*, p. 177.

15. *Idem*

16. As reported in the interview with the author at Arenys de Mar on August 3, 1965.

17. *Los cipreses*, p. 18.

18. *Ibid.*, p. 185

19. *Ibid.*, p. 257.

20. *Ibid.*, p. 291.

21. *Ibid.*, p. 238.

22. Thurston N. Davis, "Inside Spain," *America Magazine*, Vol. 93 (April 23, 1965), 105.

23. Fuertes J. Velarde, "Gironella: la segunda república y la economía española," *Correo Literario*, Madrid, Vol. 92 (Mar. 15, 1954), 8.

24. *Los cipreses*, p. 382.

25. *Ibid.*, pp. 405–6.

26. José Vila Selma, "El mundo de Gironella," *Punta Europa* (Madrid), I (1956), 128.

27. *Los cipreses*, p. 443.

28. Vila Selma, *Punta Europa*, I, 132.

29. *Los cipreses*, p. 469.

30. G. Torrente Ballester, *Panorama de la literatura contemporánea*, 2nd ed. (Madrid: Ed. Guadarrama, 1961), p. 425.

31. *Los cipreses*, p. 567.

32. *Ibid.*, p. 581.

33. *Ibid.*, p. 624.

34. Julián Marías, "Gironella y los planos de su mundo," *La Nación* (Buenos Aires, Sept. 13, 1959), p. 27.

35. Fuertes J. Velarde's article, "Gironella: la segunda república y la economía española," *Correo Literario*, Vol. 92 (Mar. 14, 1954), 8–10, is eclectic historical scholarship derived from *Los cipreses*.

36. *Los cipreses*, p. 777.

37. *Ibid.*, p. 781.

38. *Ibid.*, p. 791.

39. *Ibid.*, p. 792.

40. *Ibid.*, p. 843.

41. *Ibid.*, p. 870.

42. Sister Scholastica Schuster, "Song for a Catholic World,"

Catholic World Magazine, Vol. 183 (Spring 1956), 435.

43. J. Gich, "Libros de la quincena: *Los cipreses creen en Dios,*" *Correo Literario,* Vol. 70 (Madrid, Apr. 15, 1953), 4.

44. William J. Grupp, "José María Gironella, Spanish Novelist," *Kentucky Foreign Language Quarterly,* IV, No. 3 (1957), 33.

45. Kerrigan, *Books on Trial,* XIV, 388.

46. Mark Van Doren, "Thousand Faces of Spain," *Reporter Magazine,* XII (June 16, 1955), 36.

47. Cano, *Insula,* Vol. 89, 7.

48. Anthony West, *New Yorker,* XXXI, 122.

49. Richard Urbanski, "Revoluntionary Novels of Gironella and Pasternak," *Hispania,* XLIII (May 1960), 191–97.

50. F. G. Castro, "Situación actual de la novela española," *Indice de artes y letras* (Madrid), No. 62 (April 1953), 7.

51. Thomas C. Bergin, "Spain in Chaos," *Saturday Review,* Vol. 38 (April 16, 1955), 15.

52. Schuster, *Catholic World Magazine,* Vol. 435–36.

53. *Ibid.,* p. 436.

54. Vila Selma, *Punta Europa,* I. 128.

Chapter Five

1. José María Gironella, *Los cipreses creen en Dios* (Barcelona: Ed. Planeta, 1953), p. 537.

2. *Ibid.,* p. 846.

3. *Ibid.,* p. 843.

4. *Ibid.,* p. 842.

5. *Ibid.,* pp. 775–76.

6. *Ibid.,* p. 471.

7. *Ibid.,* pp. 870–71.

8. *Ibid.,* p. 40.

9. *Ibid.,* p. 759.

10. *Ibid.,* p. 851.

11. *Ibid.,* p. 519.

12. *Ibid.,* p. 842.

13. *Ibid.,* p. 525.

14. *Ibid.,* p. 446.

15. *Ibid.,* p. 188.

16. *Ibid.,* p. 538.

17. *Ibid.,* p. 325.

18. *Ibid.,* p. 844.

19. *Ibid.,* p. 845.

20. As reported in an interview with the author at Arenys de Mar on August 3, 1965.

21. Gironella, *Un millón de muertos* (Barcelona: Ed. Planeta, 1961), p. 10.

22. Edward J. Gramberg, "J. M. Gironella, ¿novelista?" *Cuadernos del congreso por la libertad de la cultura*, No. 79 (Dec. 1963), 66.

23. *Un millón de muertos*, p. 23.

24. *Ibid.*, pp. 23–24.

25. *Ibid.*, p. 51.

26. *Ibid.*, p. 55.

27. *Ibid.*, p. 97.

28. *Ibid.*, p. 117.

29. *Ibid.*, p. 134.

30. *Ibid.*, p. 171.

31. *Ibid.*, p. 228.

32. *Ibid.*, p. 229.

33. *Ibid.*, p. 315.

34. *Ibid.*, p. 288.

35. *Ibid.*, p. 337.

36. *Ibid.*, p. 473.

37. *Ibid.*, p. 631.

38. J. J. Devlin, "Arturo Barea and J. M. Gironella: Two Interpreters of the Spanish Labyrinth," *Hispania*, XLI (1958), 148.

39. M. Fernández Almagro, "Reseña de *Un millón de muertos*," *ABC* (Madrid, Mar. 12, 1961), Supplement.

40. Joaquín Pérez Madrigal, *España a dos voces: los infundios y la historia* (Madrid: Ed. E. A. S. A., 1961), Introduction.

41. Luis Emilio Calvo Sotelo, "Crítica y glosa de *Un millón de muertos*"; artículos publicados en *Ya* sobre la novela de J. M. Gironella (Madrid: Amigos de Calvo Sotelo, Apr. 16, 1961–June 20, 1961), Sections I, III and VIII, respectively, with no pages indicated in text.

42. *Un millón de muertos*, p. 369.

43. Richard E. Chandler and Kessel Schwartz, *A New History of Spanish Literature* (Baton Rouge: Louisiana State University Press, 1961), p. 262.

44. *Un millón de muertos*, p. 610.

45. *Ibid.*, p. 617.

46. *Ibid.*, p. 621.

47. There is an abundance of scholarly works in this field. Two recent ones, Hugh Thomas' *The Spanish Civil War*, (New York: Harper, 1961) and Robert Payne's *The Civil War In Spain* (New York: Putnam, 1962), are excellent.

48. *Un millón de muertos*, p. 684.

49. *Ibid.*, p. 731.

50. *Ibid.*, p. 768.

51. *Ibid.*, p. 762.

52. *Ibid.*, p. 777.

53. *Ibid.*, p. 788.

54. As reported in an interview with the author at Arenys de Mar on August 3, 1965.

55. José Luis Cano, "Carta de España: dos libros sobre la Guerra Civil Española," *Asomante*, XVII (1962), 60.

56. J. L. Vásquez Dodero, "El arte y la historia en *Un millón de muertos*," *Nuestro Tiempo*, XIV (1961), 740.

57. R. M. Hornedo, "José María Gironella," *Razón y fe*, CLXIV (1961), 231.

58. Gironella, "Así escribí *Un millón de muertos*," *Todos somos fugitivos* (Barcelona: Ed. Planeta, 1962), pp. 299–339.

59. *Ibid.*, pp. 303–4.

60. As reported in an interview with the author at Arenys de Mar on August 3, 1965.

61. Gironella, "Así escribí . . . ," p. 299.

62. *Ibid.*, p. 318.

63. *Ibid.*, p. 321.

64. *Idem*

65. *Ibid.*, p. 322.

66. Vásquez Dodero, *Nuestro Tiempo*, XIV, 739.

67. Gironella, "Así escribí . . . ," p. 325.

68. *Ibid.*, p. 333.

Chapter Six

1. Gironella, *Todos somos fugitivos* (Barcelona: Ed. Planeta, 1961), p. 325.

2. *Ibid.*, p. 324.

3. Gironella, *Los fantasmas de mi cerebro* (Barcelona: Ed. Planeta, 1958), p. 9.

4. *Ibid.*, p. 81.

5. *Ibid.*, p. 124.

6. *Ibid.*, p. 125.

7. *Ibid.*, p. 126.

8. *Ibid.*, p. 122.

9. *Ibid.*, p. 128.

10. *Idem*

11. *Idem*

12. *Ibid.*, p. 129.

13. *Ibid.*, p. 133.

14. *Ibid.*, p. 138.

15. *Idem*

16. *Ibid.*, p. 141.

17. *Ibid.*, p. 156.

18. *Ibid.*, p. 143.

19. *Ibid.*, p. 144.

20. *Ibid.*, p. 145.

21. *Ibid.*, p. 147.

22. *Idem*

23. *Ibid.*, p. 151.

24. *Ibid.*, p. 146.

25. *Ibid.*, p. 161.

26. *Ibid.*, p. 195.

27. *Ibid.*, p. 200.

28. *Ibid.*, p. 206.

29. José Luis Cano, "Libros del mes," *Insula,* Vol. 151 (June 15, 1959), Supplement.

30. Gironella, *Los fantasmas . . .* , p. 210.

31. Gironella, "Muerte y juicio de Giovanni Papini," *Los fantasmas . . .* , p. 30.

32. As reported in an interview with the author at Arenys de Mar, on August 3, 1965.

33. Gironella, "Carta de un gusano a Jesucristo," *Los fantasmas . . . .* , p. 69.

34. Gironella, "Meditaciones," *Los fantasmas . . .* , p. 301.

35. *Ibid.*, pp. 302–3.

36. *Ibid.*, p. 309.

37. *Ibid.*, p. 312.

38. Edward J. Gramberg, "J. M. Gironella, ¿novelista?" *Cuadernos del congreso por la libertad de la cultura,* No. 79 (Dec. 1963), 64.

39. Gironella, *Los fantasmas . . .* , p. 314.

40. *Ibid.*, p. 316.

Chapter Seven

1. Gironella, *Los fantasmas de mi cerebro* (Barcelona: Ed. Planeta, 1958), p. 205.

2. Gironella, *Phantoms and Fugitives,* trans. Terry Broch Fontseré (New York: Sheed and Ward, 1964), p. vii. Quotation is available only in English from the author's foreword written especially for this edition.

3. Fernández Cuenca, "Los escritores del día," *Bibliografía Hispánica,* XIV, No. 11 (Nov. 1955), 279.

4. Gironella, "Milagro en el pueblo," *Todos somos fugitivos* (Barcelona: Ed. Planeta, 1961), p. 57.

5. Gironella, "El suicida y su hermano," *Todos somos fugitivos,* p. 77.

6. Gironella, "La muerte del mar," *Todos somos fugitivos*, p. 91.

7. *Ibid.*, p. 100.

Chapter Eight

1. Edward J. Gramberg, "José María Gironella, ¿novelista?" *Cuadernos del congreso por la libertad de la cultura*, No. 79, 68.

2. Gironella, *Mujer, levántate y anda* (Barcelona: Ed. Planeta, 1962), Prologue.

3. *Ibid.*, p. 72.

4. *Ibid.*, pp. 113–14.

5. As reported in an interview with the author at Arenys de Mar on August 3, 1965.

6. Gironella, "Saber dudar," *Los fantasmas de mi cerebro* (Barcelona: Ed. Planeta, 1958, p. 331.

7. Gironella, "Rutas desérticas," *Los fantasmas*..., p. 334.

8. Gironella, "Los niños ricos," *Los fantasmas*..., p. 339.

9. Fortunately, this situation has radically changed since Gironella wrote his article, "Falta de imaginación." In April, 1965, a festival of New Spanish Cinema was presented at the Museum of Modern Art in New York City. Six new films were shown of which three ("Nunca pasa nada," "Diálogos de la paz," and "La tía Tula") indicated the growth of an exciting new Spanish cinema since 1950.

10. Gironella, "Escuelas mortuorias en Italia," *Los fantasmas*..., p. 224.

11. Gironella, "Temas franceses," *Los fantasmas*..., p. 252.

12. Gironella, "El mundo no se ha vuelto loco," *Los fantasmas*..., p. 283.

13. Gironella, "Una estadística sorprendente," *Los fantasmas*..., p. 286.

14. Gironella, "Un belén norteamericano en París," *Los fantasmas*..., p. 296.

15. As reported in an interview with the author at Arenys de Mar on August 3, 1965.

16. Letter from the author, July 12, 1966, in which he states he is waiting for the decision of the Censorship Bureau in Madrid before the publication of his next novel is permitted.

Chapter Nine

1. Gironella, *Personas, ideas y mares* (Barcelona: Ed. Planeta, 1963), p. 9.

2. *Ibid.*, p. 22.

3. *Ibid.*, p. 37.

4. *Ibid.*, p. 33.

5. *Idem*
6. *Ibid.*, p. 41.
7. *Ibid.*, p. 105.
8. *Ibid.*, p. 45.
9. *Ibid.*, p. 15.
10. *Ibid.*, p. 76.
11. *Ibid.*, p. 228.
12. *Ibid.*, p. 130.
13. *Ibid.*, pp. 158–59.
14. *Ibid.*, pp. 176–77, 178.
15. *Ibid.*, p. 193.
16. *Ibid.*, p. 188.
17. *Ibid.*, p. 215.
18. *Idem*
19. *Ibid.*, p. 227.
20. *Idem*
21. *Ibid.*, p. 234.
22. *Idem*
23. *Ibid.*, p. 268.
24. *Ibid.*, p. 286.
25. *Ibid.*, p. 301.
26. *Ibid.*, p. 319.
27. *Ibid.*, p. 327.
28. *Idem*
29. *Ibid.*, p. 339.
30. *Ibid.*, p. 368.
31. *Ibid.*, p. 393.
32. *Ibid.*, p. 357.
33. Gironella, *El Japón y su duende* (Barcelona: Ed. Planeta, 1964), p. 33.
34. *Ibid.*, p. 271.
35. *Ibid.*, p. 287.

Chapter Ten

1. Although the China essay originally appeared in an undated Spanish periodical entitled *Gaceta Ilustrada,* John F. Byrne thought it wise to translate and present it together with the Cuban essay in a single volume, *On China and Cuba* (Notre Dame, Indiana: Fides Publishers, Inc., 1963), to give a complete inventory of Gironella's most important political writings.
2. Gironella, "Rumbo a América," *Todos somos fugitivos* (Barcelona: Ed. Planeta, 1961), p. 104.
3. *Ibid.*, p. 105.

4. *Ibid.,* p. 106.

5. *Ibid.,* p. 136.

6. *Idem*

7. *Ibid.,* p. 137.

8. In his essay on Cuba on page 119 of John Byrne's translation of Gironella's *On China and Cuba,* the author contradicts himself. He declares that his interview with Mr. Stevenson took place but lacked the "necessary vigor so vital [in America] if we are going to give meaning and cohesion to the slippery complexity of these times." In retrospect, he relates his condemnation of the United States: "It was an unforgettable experience but, viewed as a whole, somewhat sad, since it had only confirmed my fears with respect to the myopia and immaturity of the Colossus of the West."

9. Gironella, "Las tres Europas," *Todos somos fugitivos,* p. 143.

10. Gironella, "Viaje en torno a la revolución cubana," *Todos somos fugitivos,* p. 297.

11. Gironella, *On China and Cuba,* trans. John F. Byrne, *ed. cit.,* p. vi.

12. The original Spanish edition is out of print and unavailable. Therefore quotations from Byrne's version in English appear in the text.

13. Gironella, *On China and Cuba,* p. vii.

14. *Ibid.,* p. 47.

15. Gironella, *China, lágrima inumerable* (Barcelona: Ed. Planeta, 1965), p. 24.

16. *Ibid.,* p. 183.

17. *Ibid.,* p. 215.

18. *Ibid.,* p. 220.

Chapter Eleven

1. Gironella, "¿Por qué el mundo desconoce la novela española?," *Los fantasmas de mi cerebro* (Barcelona: Ed. Planeta, 1958), p. 392.

2. Edmund Urbanski, "El revisionismo en la valoración de las letras y cultura contemporánea de España," *Hispania,* XLVIII (December 1965), 820–21.

3. Gironella, "Confesiones de un escritor," *Los fantasmas . . . ,* p. 396.

4. *Ibid.,* p. 397.

5. As reported in an interview with the author at Arenys de Mar on August 3, 1965.

6. Gramberg, "José María Gironella, ¿novelista?" *Cuadernos del congreso por la libertad de la cultura,* No. 79 (December 1963), 65.

7. Gironella, "Narciso Yepes, guitarrista," *Todos somos fugitivos* (Barcelona: Ed. Planeta, 1961), p. 175.

8. *Ibid.*, p. 180.

9. *Ibid.*, p. 186.

10. Gironella, "Julián Marías, filósofo y articulista," *Los fantasmas* . . . , p. 356.

11. Gironella, "Confesiones de un escritor," *Todos somos fugitivos,* p. 205.

12. *Ibid.*, p. 203.

13. As reported in an interview with the author at Arenys de Mar on August 3, 1965.

14. At the time of the interview, Gironella was engrossed in reading Enrique Salgado's *El mundo de los miopes.*

15. As reported in an interview with the author at Arenys de Mar on August 3, 1965.

16. Gironella, "Así escribí *un millón de muertos,*" *Todos somos fugitivos,* p. 310.

Chapter Twelve

1. Gironella, *Ha estallado la paz* (Barcelona: Ed. Planeta, 1966), p. 9.

2. *Ibid.*, p. 17.

3. *Ibid.*, p. 11.

4. *Ibid.*, pp. 447–48.

Chapter Thirteen

1. Gironella, "Hablemos otra vez del arte moderno," *Gritos del mar* (Barcelona: Ed. Planeta, 1967), p. 269.

2. *Idem*

3. Gironella, "Barcelona y el templo de la unidad cristiana," *Gritos* . . . , p. 377.

4. Gironella, *Gritos del mar,* p. 7.

5. Gironella, "No sabemos nada," *Gritos* . . . , p. 61.

6. Gironella, "Seamos hermanos, pero no Siameses," *Gritos* . . . , p. 76.

7. Gironella, "La novela, ¿género agotado?" *Gritos* . . . , p. 167.

8. *Ibid.*, p. 166.

9. *Ibid.*, p. 168.

10. Gironella, "¿Es femenino el pueblo español?," *Gritos* . . . , p. 176.

11. Gironella, "La muerte puede ser un pseudónimo," *Gritos* . . . , p. 221.

12. Gironella, "Modesto homenaje a un amigo de Asia," *Gritos* . . . , p. 227.

13. Gironella, "La Federació de Joves Cristians de Catalunya," *Gritos* . . . , p. 235.

14. *Ibid.*, p. 239.

15. Gironella, "Antonio Taipés," *Gritos* . . . , p. 267.

16. Gironella, "Retirarse a tiempo," *Gritos* . . . , p. 149.

17. Gironella, "A la escucha del comunismo," *Gritos* . . . , p. 441.

18. Gironella, "Carta a los médicos," *Gritos* . . . , p. 346.

19. Gironella, *En Asia se muere bajo las estrellas* (Barcelona: Plaza & Janes, S. A., 1968), p. 86.

20. *Ibid.*, p. 438.

21. *Ibid.*, p. 15.

22. *Ibid.*, p. 66.

23. *Ibid.*, pp. 112–13.

24. *Ibid.*, p. 384.

25. *Ibid.*, p. 116.

Chapter Fourteen

1. In Arenys de Mar on August 3, 1965, Gironella was busily re-editing the third and final volume to date of his trilogy, *Ha estallado la paz* and inserted further dialogue and action to prepare it for a film scenario.

2. Gironella, *Todos somos fugitivos* (Barcelona: Ed. Planeta, 1961), p. 329.

3. As reported in an interview with the author at Arenys de Mar on August 3, 1965.

4. Juan Luis Alborg, *Hora actual de la novela española* (Madrid: Ed. Taurus, 1958), p. 155.

5. William J. Grupp, "José María Gironella, Spanish Novelist," *Kentucky Foreign Language Quarterly*, IV, No. 3 (1957), 135.

Selected Bibliography

PRIMARY SOURCES

1. Original Works by José María Gironella

Ha llegado el invierno y tú no estás aquí (Barcelona: Entregas de poesía, 1945). Out of print.

Un hombre (Barcelona: Ed. Destino, 1946).

La marea (Barcelona: Ed. Planeta, 1949).

Los cipreses creen en Dios (Barcelona: Ed. Planeta, 1953).

El novelista ante el mundo (Madrid: Ed. Rialp, 1954). Out of print.

Los fantasmas de mi cerebro (Barcelona: Ed. Planeta, 1958).

Muerte y juicio de Giovanni Papini (Barcelona: Ed. Planeta, 1959). Out of print. Usually included in *Los fantasmas de mi cerebro*.

Un millón de muertos (Barcelona: Ed. Planeta, 1961).

Todos somos fugitivos (Barcelona: Ed. Planeta, 1961).

Mujer, levántate y anda (Barcelona: Ed. Planeta, 1962).

Personas, ideas y mares (Barcelona: Ed. Planeta, 1963).

El Japón y su duende (Barcelona: Ed. Planeta, 1964).

China, lágrima innumerable (Barcelona: Ed. Planeta, 1965).

Ha estallado la paz (Barcelona: Ed. Planeta, 1966).

Gritos del mar (Barcelona: Ed. Planeta, 1967).

En Asia se muere bajo las estrellas (Barcelona: Plaza & Janes, 1968).

2. Translations

The Cypresses Believe in God. Translated by Harriet de Onís (New York: Alfred E. Knopf, 1955).

Where the Soil Was Shallow. Translated by Anthony Kerrigan (Chicago: Henry Regnery Co., 1957).

One Million Dead. Translated by Joan MacLean (New York: Doubleday, 1963).

On China and Cuba. Translation with Prologue by John F. Byrne (Notre Dame, Indiana: Fides Publishers Inc., 1963).

SECONDARY SOURCES

1. Books

ALBORG, JUAN L. *Hora actual de la novela española* (Madrid: Ed. Taurus, 1958). Verbose but comprehensive critical work of today's leading Spanish novelists.

BARZUN, JACQUES. *Classic, Romantic and Modern* (New York: Double-day-Anchor Books, 1961). Excellent background material, including definitions of genres.

CHANDLER, RICHARD E. and KESSEL SCHWARTZ. *A New History of Spanish Literature* (Baton Rouge: Louisiana State University Press, 1961). The best literary history of Spain to date; the authors recognize and are gratified by Gironella's sizeable contributions to explain the political entanglements of the Civil War.

HOYOS, ANTONIO DE. *Ocho escritores actuales* (Murcia: Aula de cultura, 1954). A fair accounting of eight modern Spanish writers, including Gironella whom he admires.

MADARIAGA, SALVADOR DE. *Ingleses, franceses, españoles* (Buenos Aires: Ed. Sudamericana, 1958). Perceptive study of the English, French, and Spanish character; probably read by Gironella and used as a basis for many of his "sociological" essays.

MARIN, DIEGO and DEL RIO, ANGEL. *Breve historia de la literatura española* (New York: Holt, Rinehart and Winston, 1966). Particularly good history of the twentieth century and its writers with a somewhat sketchy outline of Gironella and his works.

MICHENER, JAMES A. *Iberia: Spanish Travels and Reflections* (New York: Random House, 1968). A rambling, chatty work containing some relevant information on Spain's contemporary novelists including Gironella and his problems with publishers.

NORA, EUGENIO G. DE. *La novela española contemporánea* Vol. II Pt. II (Madrid: Ed. Gredos, 1962). A detailed history with excellent bibliographies of writers.

PAYNE, ROBERT. *The Civil War in Spain* (New York: Putnam, 1962). Good background material to aid in understanding Gironella based on eyewitness accounts.

PEREZ MADRIGAL, JOAQUIN. *España a dos voces: los infundios y la historia* (Madrid: Ed. E. A. S. A., 1961). A heavy, intellectually pompous, pseudo-historical work.

PEREZ MINIK, DOMINGO. *Novelistas españoles de los siglos XIX y XX* (Madrid: Ed. Guadarrama, 1957). Excellent study of modern novelists but currently out of print.

SAINZ DE ROBLES, FEDERICO CARLOS. *La novela española en el siglo XX* (Madrid: Ed. Pegaso, 1957). Fair appraisal of the genre but written in weighty prose.

THOMAS HUGH. *The Spanish Civil War* (New York: Harper, 1961). The best history of its kind; excellent as background for Gironella.

TORRENTE BALLESTER, GONZALO. *Panorama de la literature contemporánea* (Madrid: Ed. Guadarrama, 1961). Short biographical accounts of writers in all genres with valuable bibliography.

1967 edition is much improved by cutting selections from the writers' works and expanding criticism of their abilities.

VALBUENA PRAT, ANGEL. *Historia de la literature española* (Barcelona: Ed. Gustavo Gili, S. A., 1957). A standard history; sometimes there are penetrating insights into modern authors although for Gironella, he is merely mentioned as promising.

ZAMARRIEGO, TOMAS. *Tipología sacerdotal en la novela española contemporánea: Bernanos, Mauriac, Gironella* (Madrid: Ed. Razón y fe, 1959). Excellent thesis transformed into short book of criticism. Particularly good thoughts on the French novelists and on Gironella's conceptions of the priesthood.

2. Articles and Periodicals

ALBORG, JUAN L. "Los novelistas: José María Gironella," *Indice de artes y letras,* No. 94 (Oct. 1956), 9. Some important biographical details are included.

ANGELES, JOSE. "Review of Gironella's *Ha estallado la paz*" in *Books Abroad.* University of Oklahoma Press, Vol. 41 No. 4 (Autumn 1967), p. 451. A fairly concise and competent appraisal of a very long novel.

BERGIN, THOMAS C. "Spain in Chaos," *Saturday Review,* Vol. 38 (April 16, 1955), 14–15. Competent review of *The Cypresses Believe in God.*

BOYLE, KAY. "Spain Divided," *Nation,* Vol. 180 (June 11,, 1955), 506–7. A study of *The Cypresses* full of insights into Spain and her people by a leading American short story writer.

CALVO SOTELO, LUIS EMILIO. "Crítica y glosa de *Un millón de muertos,*" *Ya* (Apr. 16, 1961-June 30, 1961), articles unnumbered. Incisive criticism of *One Million Dead* by the son of Calvo Sotelo, sometimes at odds with Gironella's interpretations of history.

CANO, JOSE LUIS. "Los libros del mes: *Un hombre* de Gironella," *Insula,* Vol. 18 (June 15, 1947), 5. Competent review stressing promising career of new writer.

————. "Los libros del mes: *La marea* por Gironella," *Insula,* Vol. 49 (Jan. 15, 1950), 4. Competent review of a poor novel.

————. "Los libros del mes: *Los cipreses creen en Dios* por Gironella," *Insula,* Vol. 89 (May 1953), 6–7. Laudatory review of Gironella's best novel to date.

————. "Los libros del mes: *Los fantasmas de mi cerebro* por Gironella," *Insula,* Vol. 151 (June 15, 1959), supplement. Review of Gironella's hassle with his own psyche.

CANO, JOSE LUIS. "Carta de España: dos libros sobre la guerra civil española," *Asomante,* Vol. XVII (1962), 59–61. Cano reviews the leading novels on the Spanish Civil War.

CASTRO, F. G. DE. "Situación actual de la novela española (comentario sobre la obra de Gironella)," *Indice de artes y letras,* No. 62 (Apr. 1953), 7–8. Competent review of Gironella's *The Cypresses Believe in God.*

CLANCY, WILLIAM J. "Review of *The Cypresses Believe in God,*" *Commonweal,* LXII (Apr. 15, 1955), 53. The *Cypresses* viewed as a "religious" novel.

COLOMER, EUSEBIO. "Reseña: *Un millón de muertos,*" *Razón y fe,* CLXIII (1961), 483–94. Undistinguished review of Gironella's second war novel.

CUENCA, M. FERNANDEZ. "Los escritores del día," *Bibliografía Hispánica,* XIV (Nov. 1955), 279. Some good insights from Cuenca's interview with Gironella.

DAVIS, THURSTON N. "Inside Spain," *America,* Vol. 93 (Aug. 23, 1955), 104–5. An adequate review of literary circles, events in modern Spain.

DEVLIN, J. J. "Arturo Barea and J. M. Gironella: Two Interpreters of the Spanish Labyrinth," *Hispania,* XLI (1958), 143–48. Excellent article about Barea and Gironella as interpreters of the Civil War.

FERNANDEZ ALMAGRO, M. "Reseña de *Un millón de muertos,*" *ABC,* Madrid (Mar. 12, 1961), supplement. A good appraisal of Gironella's second war novel.

GARCIA-LUENGO, EUSEBIO. "Gironella tardíamente. *Los cipreses creen en Dios,*" *Indice de artes y letras,* No. 64 (June 30, 1953), supplement. Competent review tracing growth of Gironella's career.

GICH, J. "Los libros de quincena: *Los cipreses creen en Dios,*" *Correo Literario,* No. 70 (April 15, 1953), 4. Adequate review with intelligent insights into novelist and his problems.

GOMEZ DE LA SERNA, GASPAR. "Reseña de *Los cipreses creen en Dios,*" *Clavileño,* No. 22 (July-August, 1953), 70–71. Adequate review of Gironella's career.

————. "El nuevo episodio de J. M. Gironella," *España en sus episodios nacionales,* Madrid: Ed. del Movimiento (1954), 199–236. Excellent appraisal of Gironella's intended use of his war novels.

GRAMBERG, EDWARD J. "J. M. Gironella ¿novelista?" *Cuadernos del congreso por la libertad de la cultura,* No. 79 (Dec. 1963), 62–68. Penetrating analysis of Gironella's career, stressing his merits as a writer.

GRUPP, WILLIAM J. "J. M. Gironella, Spanish Novelist," *Kentucky Foreign Language Quarterly,* IV, No. 3 (1957), 129–35. A competent appraisal of a young writer and his novels before 1955.

HORNEDO, RAFAEL MARIA. "José María Gironella," *Razón y fe*, CLXIV (1961), 222–31. Some interesting thoughts come from Gironella himself in this interview.

KERRIGAN, ANTHONY. "J. M. Gironella and the Black Legend of Spain," *Books on Trial*, XIV (Apr.-May 1956), 343–45. An excellent treatise on the Civil War by Gironella's leading translator.

KLIBBE, LAWRENCE H. "Gironella's *Where the Soil Was Shallow*," *Catholic World*, Vol. 188 (Feb. 1959), 399–402. A competent review stressing the "religious elements" of Gironella's novel.

MARIAS, JULIAN. "Gironella y los planos de su mundo," *La nación*, Buenos Aires (Sept. 13, 1959), 27. Marías understands Gironella's conscientious desire to write war novels true to a well-planned integration of history and fiction.

SCHEVILL, ISABEL MAGANA. "A Day with Gironella," *Hispania*, XLII (May 1959), 170–74. A pleasant interview in which the author speaks to Gironella about Spain and listens to his answers on contemporary problems of Spanish writers.

SCHUSTER, SISTER SCHOLASTICA. "Song for a Catholic World," *Catholic World*, Vol. 183 (Spring 1956), 433–36. *The Cypresses* is viewed as a "Catholic" novel.

URBANSKI, EDMUND STEPHEN. "Revolutionary Novels of Gironella and Pasternak," *Hispania*, XLIII (May 1960), 191–97. A strikingly good comparison of Gironella and Pasternak, with Gironella holding his own.

————. 'El revisionismo en la valoración de las letras y cultura contemporánea de España," *Hispania*, XLVIII (Dec. 1965), 816–25. Gironella's role as social pace-setter, critic.

VAN DOREN, MARK. "Thousand Faces of Spain," *Reporter*, Vol. 12 (June 16, 1955), 35–37. An excellent analysis of *The Cypresses Believe in God*.

VASQUEZ DODERO, J. L. "Sentido de una novela," *Nuestro Tiempo* (Feb. 8, 1955), 110. A judicious, well thought out appraisal of *The Cypresses Believe in God*.

————. "El arte y la historia en *Un millón de muertos*," *Nuestro Tiempo*, XIV (1961), 732–42. A fairly competent review that attempts to relate art and history as Gironella uses them in his novels.

VELARDE, FUERTES J. "Gironella, la Segunda República y la economía española," *Correo Literario*, Vol. 92 (Mar. 1954), 8–9. Strictly for readers who care to check the validity of Gironella's statistics of Spain's economy; has nothing to do with Gironella's fictional works.

VILA SELMA, JOSE. "El mundo de Gironella," *Punta Europa*, I (1956), 128–35. Helpful article on Gironella's literary purpose.

WEST, ANTHONY. "Review of *The Cypresses Believe in God*," *New Yorker*, Vol. 31 (May 28, 1955), 120–22. An excellent appraisal of *The Cypresses* by an American writer.

New Bibliography

The following titles of Gironella and critical works were published after type-setting and their evalution could not be included in this book:

1. *Books*

GIRONELLA, JOSE MARIA. *Conversaciones con Don Juan de Borbón* (Madrid: Ed. Afrodisio Aguado, 1968). Published in a limited edition, this small volume was not available in the United States until recently.

————. *Peace After War*. Translated by Joan MacLean (New York: Alfred A. Knopf, 1969). This is the English version of Gironella's *Ha estallado la paz*, whose English title avoids the irony of the Spanish original.

————. *Gritos de la tierra* (Barcelona: Ed. Planeta, 1970). Another of Gironella's collections of newspaper and magazine articles similar to *Gritos del mar*.

————. *Los hombres lloran solos* (Barcelona: Ed. Planeta, 1971). The fourth volume of Gironella's "pentology" about Spain's Civil War.

2. *Articles and Periodicals*

BOTANA, JOSE. "José María Gironella: Nuevos episodios nacionales," *Duquesne Hispanic Review*, 6, iii (1967), 13–33. Another worthwhile look into Gironella's Civil War trilogy.

GALLAGHER, DAVID. "Review of *Peace After War*," *New York Times Book Review*, (June 1, 1969), 4. An extremely competent appraisal of this continuation of Gironella's Civil War novels.

PAYNE, ROBERT. "Review of *Peace After War*," *Saturday Review of Literature*, 52, (May 17, 1969), 49. A penetrating analysis of Gironella's strengths and weaknesses as a novelist.

STEEL, B. D. "A New *Loísta*: J. M. Gironella," *Hispania* XLI (1968), 866–67. Gironella's use of *lo* in an examination of his prose style.

Index